JAPAN
THROUGH
CHILDREN'S
LITERATURE

JAPAN THROUGH CHILDREN'S LITERATURE

An Annotated Bibliography

An Enlarged Second Edition

Compiled by YASUKO MAKINO
With the assistance of ROBERTA K. GUMPORT

Greenwood Press

Westport, Connecticut • London, England

Library of Congress Cataloging-in-Publication Data

Makino, Yasuko.
  Japan through children's literature.

  Includes indexes.
    1. Japan—Bibliography—Juvenile literature.
  2. Children's literature—Bibliography. I. Gumport,
  Roberta K. II. Title.
  Z3306.M34 1985 [DS806]   016.952   85-21941
  ISBN 0-313-24611-4 (lib. bdg. : alk. paper)

Library of Congress Catalog Card Number: 85-21941
ISBN: 0-313-24611-4

First published in 1985

Greenwood Press
A division of Congressional Information Service, Inc.
88 Post Road West, Westport, Connecticut 06881

Printed in the United States of America

∞™

The paper used in this book complies with the
Permanent Paper Standard issued by the National
Information Standards Organization (Z39.48-1984).

10 9 8 7 6 5 4 3 2 1

CONTENTS

PREFACE

The idea for this bibliography was first conceived while I was taking a children's literature course in library school some fifteen years ago. Lois Scholtz, the instructor, encouraged me to polish for publication my paper about Japanese folklore for children. I never got around to doing it, but I kept on reading books on Japan written for children and taking notes. By 1977, I had accumulated enough material for a book, and with strong encouragement from people who had used my manuscript bibliography for workshops on Japan, I approached the Asia Society in New York. Dr. Betty Bullard, then Director of the Society's Education Department, read the manuscript and kindly hunted for a publisher. She arranged to have it published as an Occasional Paper by the Center for International Studies at Duke University, using a publication subsidy from the Asia Society.

This bibliography has been out of print for some time, and the Center for International Studies at Duke has gone through an organizational change and does not intend to publish a new edition. Consequently I requested permission to use the material for a new edition. For this new edition, I have enlarged the scope of the work to include material appropriate for high school level courses. I have retained the original title although it now covers a wider range of children's literature.

Japan Through Children's Literature is intended to help young Americans acquire an accurate image and understanding of Japanese culture. I have used children's literature as a vehicle to accomplish my goal, for I thought young Americans could easily identify with their counterparts in these stories. This new edition evaluates trade books on Japan in order to help teachers, librarians, and interested parents in the United States select materials from the vast numbers of books available. Its scope is fairly comprehensive for trade books published in English from the mid-sixties to date. Some of the books, primarily on social studies, which were included in the first edition have been deleted from this edition because the information has become obsolete and new books in the same subject area have been

published. I have also included books published in the fifties and
early sixties provided they are still in print or available in many
libraries.

There are many books for children published each year in Japan,
and more and more of these are being translated and made available in
this country. For the present purpose, however, I have limited the
materials to those which could be used to teach Japanese culture to
young Americans. For this reason, I did not include books on
Japanese-Americans.

Each book is evaluated in terms of content and accuracy in
portraying Japan, its culture and people. A suggested grade level for
each work is indicated at the end of the bibliographic data.
Annotations are divided by subject, and cross references are supplied
for books belonging to more than one subject area. Books which are
listed in reference sources under the subject heading of "Japan," but
which really have nothing to do with the country are listed at the
end of each chapter so that readers will not waste time looking for
them.

It is my hope that this critical bibliography will make a modest
contribution toward informing young Americans, as well as their
teachers and librarians, about Japan and its people and will help the
communications gap between these two countries.

My grateful acknowledgment and thanks go to a number of people
and institutions which made this work possible: Dr. Betty Bullard who
made the publication of the first edition possible; the Interlibrary
Loan Department of the University of Illinois at Urbana-Champaign
Library which serviced my numerous requests over the years; the
Center for East Asian and Pacific Studies of the University of
Illinois which provided me with a travel grant for my trip to the New
York Public Library and to the Library of Congress; the Research and
Publication Committee of the University of Illinois Library for its
financial assistance; Mr. Michael Gorman, Director of General
Services of the University of Illinois Library who encouraged me to
approach publishers for this new edition and also granted me a leave
of absence to work on this project; the generous publishers who
either supplied books or information about their publications; the
editorial staff of Greenwood Press; and my typist Ms. Sonya Davidson.
Finally, I must express my deepest appreciation to Mrs. Roberta K.
Gumport, who not only edited the text but also made a number of
valuable suggestions concerning the contents and the arrangement of
this bibliography. She is a doctoral student majoring in Chinese
history, with a minor in Japanese history, and has taught Chinese and
Japanese history at the University High School of the University of
Illinois. She is also the mother of two teenagers. Because of Mrs.
Gumport's excellent qualifications and background, she was my best
critic. I feel extremely lucky to have had her assistance at the
crucial stages of assembling the materials for this work. Needless to
say, I am entirely responsible for whatever defects remain in this
bibliography.

INTRODUCTION

When I first came to the United States in 1964, Americans knew little about Japan and asked me many questions. "Are there department stores in Japan?" "Do they make cars in Japan?" "Are there telephones in Japan?" One person even asked me if I had come from Japan by bus! When I asked where I could buy soy beans, people laughed and asked me if I had cows to feed.

After twenty years, Japanese cars are all over (many Americans think there are too many of them). Soy beans, in the form of soy meal, are in one of the most American of foods, hamburgers, and <u>tofu</u>, soy bean cake, is sold in most supermarkets. There is also a regular program on national television entitled "This Week in Japan."

Things have certainly changed, but I fear they have not changed enough. There are still mistakes about Japanese culture and society in children's books published in the 1970s and 1980s, although information is available to the authors, illustrators, and publishers. Many people still make incorrect assumptions such as believing that Japanese books always start from the back, that Japanese of both sexes bathe together in public bathhouses, or that the Japanese bow whenever they speak to one another as we often see on television commercials or in bad movies.

One of the most frequently misunderstood Japanese customs has to do with forms of address. Many Americans think that Japanese add <u>san</u>, an honorific for names, to any name or title. <u>San</u> is in many ways similar to the English titles "Mr.", "Mrs." or "Miss" and is a sign of respect. It is used with surnames and first names, and is attached to some nouns describing professions, occupations and stores such as <u>uekiya-san</u> (gardener) when used as a form of address or when speaking about the practitioner. It has been incorporated into certain other standard forms of address such as speaking to one's own mother and father--<u>okaasan</u> and <u>otoosan</u>, respectively. (Other words are used when referring to your mother or father.) Translating okaasan as mama-san would seem to suggest the respect of the Japanese original, but mama-san actually has a totally different meaning in Japanese. It is a term used to address bar hostesses. It would be more accurate to simply use the word "mother."

There are also several other aspects of Japanese culture and language which is difficult to express in English. The Japanese language has many different levels of speech depending on who is talking to whom. Depending on the situation, one has to change the style of one's speech and even the vocabulary. Japanese is also a gender-conscious language. Certain words and styles are used only by men or only by women. For example, interjections such as "ara" or "maa" are used only by women, while only men use "oh" or "yaa."

When you find new works on Japan which are not included in this critical bibliography, how can you tell whether they are good books? After reading this bibliography I hope you will have acquired enough knowledge to be able to tell the good books from the bad. In general, check the qualifications of the author and the illustrator, which are normally included on the cover or the frontsheets of the book. Check the text for stereotypical phrases such as "Ah-so" or "Honorable so-and-so." If the story is an adaptation or retelling, check to see if there is translation of the original and compare to see how close the adaptation comes to the original.

If you have questions about the work, contact one of the many Japanese studies programs at local colleges and universities or the cultural officers at the Japanese embassy or consulate. Addresses can be obtained through your local library. An excellent source of information is Focus on Asian Studies published by the Asia Society of New York. It is specifically aimed at educators, librarians, and professionals and includes articles on the art, history, culture, and literature of Asia as well as many book reviews. Outreach programs at many universities and colleges can also provide excellent materials. I hope that in a small way this book will help expand your knowledge about Japan and its culture.

JAPAN
THROUGH
CHILDREN'S
LITERATURE

1. ART

1-001.   Alden, Carella. Sunrise Island: A Story of Japan and its
         Arts. Art Tells a Story Series. New York: Parents'
         Magazine Press, c. 1971. 64 p. (5-9)

         This book is based on the Japanese exhibit in a series of
         exhibitions for young people entitled Arts Entertainments
         presented at the Metropolitan Museum of Art in New York. It
         presents the art of Japan from earliest times to the mid-
         nineteenth century and traces the influence of Japanese art
         on Western artists. Abundantly illustrated with an excellent
         selection of art, most owned by the Metropolitan Museum of
         Art. Some of the illustrations are in color. Readable; good
         text.

1-002.   Araki, Chiyo. Origami for Christmas. Introduction by Lillian
         Oppenheimer. New York: Kodansha International, c. 1983.
         148 p. (All ages)

         East meets West, literally, in this book on origami as the
         most delicate traditional Japanese craft of paper folding
         and the most Western of holidays, Christmas, are united.
         Twelve clear and beautiful color plates of origami
         arrangements for Christmas begin the book. The first part of
         the book has detailed step-by-step instructions for each of
         the origami. The second part details the elements, materials
         needed, and instructions for assembling the arrangements.
         Highly recommended for all ages.

1-003.   ------------. Origami in the Classroom. Rutland, VT: Tuttle,
         c. 1965. 2 v. (K-6)

Easy origami for American holidays. Can be used to show
children this traditional Japanese art of paper folding in
connection with American holidays. A suggested grade level
is indicated for each origami.

1-004.   Batterberry, Michael. Chinese and Oriental Art. Discovering
      Art Series. New York: McGraw-Hill, c. 1968. 192 p. (5 up)

This excellent art history book covers Chinese, Japanese,
and other Oriental fine arts and architecture from earliest
times to the present. It covers Japanese art only up to the
18th century, but a good portion of the book is devoted to
Japanese art. Includes over 380 excellent illustrations all
in color. Appended with a detailed index and with a list of
illustrations and the present location of the art
illustrated.

1-005.   Fukuda, Ken'ichi. Sunny Origami. Maebashi, Gunma: Jomo
      Kagaku Kogyosha, distributed by San Francisco: Japan
      Publications Trading, c. 1972. Unpaged. (K-9)

Although traditional origami utilizes square paper, in
recent years round paper origami has been developed in
Japan. This book is dedicated to this new art form.
Instructions for folding are shown on one page, and an
actual sample of the origami is pasted on the adjoining
page. Good for art classes.

1-006.   Glubok, Shirley. The Art of Japan. Special photography by
      Alfred Tamarin. New York: Macmillan, 1970. 48 p. (4-6)

This good introductory work is a comprehensive survey of
Japanese art from antiquity to the eighteenth century. The
author introduces young readers to Japanese art and shows
how it delineates the history and culture of the country.
Sections on sculpture, painting, architecture, and
landscaping are included. The only shortcoming of this book
is that no art of the modern period is included.

1-007.   Gray, Alice and Kasahara, Kunihiko, with cooperation of
      Lillian Oppenheimer and Origami Center of America. The
      Magic of Origami. Tokyo: Japan Publications, distributed
      by Japan Publications Trading, c. 1977. 132 p. (All ages)

This book is a good combination of traditional and new
origami. Origami terminology is explained and there are
clear instructions on how to decipher origami directions,
information on what kind of paper to use, and suggestions on
how to use the finished products. Detailed and easy-to-
follow directions, many accompanied by black and white
photographs of finished products.

1-008.   Harbin, Robert. <u>Origami: A Step-by-Step Guide</u>. New York:
          Hamlyn, c. 1974. 77 p. (All ages)

          Easy-to-follow step-by-step instructions for over thirty
          different <u>origami</u>, some simple and some extremely intricate.
          The directions are accompanied by color photographs of the
          completed pieces. This extremely good book includes a
          bibliography and an index.

1-009.   <u>Heibonsha Survey of Japanese Art</u>. New York:
          Weatherhill/Heibonsha, 197-- 31 v. (10 up)

          This series constitutes a full survey of Japanese art. Each
          volume treats a different topic and is written by
          specialists in that area. Each volume includes many
          illustrations in both color and black and white and an easy
          to read text. Volume 31 is an index of Japanese art.

1-010.   Hempel, Rose. <u>The Golden Age of Japan 794-1192</u>. Translated
          by Katherine Watson. New York: Rizzoli, c. 1983. 251 p.
          (10 up)

          This is a translation from the German of <u>Japan zur Heian
          Zeit</u>. The book deals, in detail, with the great Heian period
          when Japanese art and literature flourished. Heian produced
          many literary classics, many of them written by women.
          Various forms of art were also started and elaborated during
          this period. Photographs of architecture, statues,
          paintings, various art objects and calligraphy are
          abundantly included in this work. Each photograph is
          accompanied with a good, detailed explanation. The book is
          divided into four major parts: Japan as the client of
          Chinese culture; Japan's culture in transition; the
          flowering of the Heian period; and literature and life as
          reflected in paintings. This book, as well as being an art
          book, is a good source of information about this early
          period of Japanese history. It is appended with extensive
          notes, various genealogical tables, a glossary, a good
          bibliography, and an extensive index.

1-011.   Hirayama, Hakuho. <u>Sumi-E: Just for You</u>. New York: Kodansha
          International, c. 1979. 96 p. (6 up)

          Practical, easy to follow instructions for beginners of
          "One-brush" <u>sumi-e</u>. The background, technique, and spiritual
          posture which the artist should assume in order to draw
          pictures which express the spiritual beauty (essence) and
          not merely the physical beauty of the object painted are
          explained. Techniques are explained in detail and are
          accompanied by clear, large illustrations and photographs.

Suggestions for putting sumi-e paintings to practical use are included as well as samples of greeting cards and T-shirts.

1-012.   Honda, Isao. All about Origami. Tokyo: Toto Bunka, distributed by Japan Publications Trading, c. 1960. 196 p. (All ages)

Over one hundred and forty origami projects are illustrated in this excellent book. The book includes very simple to very complicated paper foldings, all with easy to follow step-by-step instructions and with photographs of the finished products. Highly recommended.

1-013.   ------------. How to Make Origami: The Japanese Art of Paper Folding. An Astor Book. New York: McDowell, Obolensky, c. 1959. 37 p. (All ages)

Clear step-by-step directions for fifteen origami, many of them animals, are given and a finished model is pasted in the book opposite the directions. The book includes an introduction to the history of origami by Lilian Oppenheimer, founder of the Origami Center in New York.

1-014.   ------------. The World of Origami. San Francisco: Japan Publications Trading, c. 1969. 264 p. (2 up)

A well-organized book that includes a good introduction to the origins of origami and what origami is. Contains clear and attractive color photographs and detailed, easy-to-follow instructions for folding. Especially useful for teachers.

1-015.   Kasahara, Kunihiko. Creative Origami. Tokyo: Japan Publications, distributed by Japan Publications Trading, c. 1967, paperback ed. 1977. 176 p. (All ages)

The book begins with an explanation of the folding techniques and symbols used in origami. Instructions for individual origami figures are grouped into categories, e.g., birds, mammals, masks, people, etc., and are often accompanied by photographs of the completed figures. Highly recommended for the advanced origami lover.

1-016.   Michener, James A. Japanese Prints: From the Early Masters to the Modern. Rutland, VT: Tuttle, published with the cooperation of the Honolulu Academy of Arts, c. 1959. 287 p. (9 up)

Over two hundred and fifty Japanese woodblock prints (about one-fifth of them in color) by more than seventy artists are included in this large-sized book. There is a good

introduction which provides extensive background
information. The prints are grouped by period into four
sections: the early prints; full-color prints; landscape and
figure prints; and modern prints. Excellent notes on the
prints and a short biography of each artist are included. A
bibliography and an extensive index. Now a little outdated,
but still usable.

1-017.   Momiyama, Nanae. Sumi-E: An Introduction to Ink Painting.
         Rutland, VT: Tuttle, c. 1967. 41 p. (7 up)

         This small book on sumi-e, or ink and brush painting,
         explains the techniques and tools of sumi-e and its history
         and philosophy as well.

1-018.   Moore, Janet Gaylord. The Eastern Gate: An Invitation to the
         Arts of China and Japan. Cleveland: Collins, c. 1979. 296
         p. (10 up)

         This book addresses the need of Westerners to distinguish
         between Chinese and Japanese arts. The two artistic
         traditions are compared and characterized. Japanese art is
         considered asymmetrical, intimate, and informal; Chinese art
         is symmetrical, in scale, and formal. The influence of
         Chinese art on Japanese art and Japanese art on Western art
         are discussed and illustrated. Historical, social,
         religious, and literary background important for the
         understanding of the artistic tradition is also included.
         Appended with notes, a list of illustrations, extensive book
         list for further reading, chronology, glossary, and index.

1-019.   Munsterberg, Hugo. The Folk Arts of Japan. Published with
         the cooperation of the Japan Society, Inc. New York,
         Rutland, VT: Tuttle, 1958. 168 p. (10-12)

         Considered by Soetsu Yanagi, the founding father of the
         Japanese folk art movement, to be the most authoritative
         work in English on folk arts in Japan. Folk art is defined
         as the "indigenous creation of the ordinary people." All
         aspects of folk art are covered including pottery,
         metalware, toys, painting and sculpture, and architecture.
         The first chapter is an excellent introduction to the field.
         The illustrations, primarily black-and-white photographs,
         are accompanied by a short explanation and an indication of
         the place of origin of the article under consideration.

1-020.   Murray, William D. and Rigney, Francis J. Paper Folding for
         Beginners. Revised ed. New York: Dover Publications, c.
         1960. 94 p. (All ages)

This is the revised edition of the 1928 publication Fun with
Paper Folding. Easy-to-follow instructions for forty-one
paper foldings are included. Many are traditional foldings.

1-021.   Noma, Seiroku. The Art of Japan. Photographs by Bin
Takahashi. New York: Kodansha International, c. 1966-1967.
1980 printing. 2 v. (10 up)

> v.1. The Art of Japan: Ancient and Medieval. Translated and
> adapted by John Rosenfield.
>
> v.2. The Art of Japan: Late Medieval to Modern. Translated
> and adapted by Glenn T. Webb.

This is an extensive work of high quality by one of the top
Japanese art historians. The work has been translated and
adapted for the Western reader. Many forms of visual arts
are discussed and their common characteristics noted.
Historical background is also included. Illustrations are
accompanied by detailed notes and supplementary notes for
each illustration are included at the end of the volume.
Both volumes have a chronology of Japanese art, a selected
bibliography, maps, and indices.

1-022.   Rathbun, William Jay. Yo no Bi: The Beauty of Japanese Folk
Art. Seattle: University of Washington Press & Seattle Art
Museum, 1983. ix, 133 p. (7 up)

This is an extensive catalog of an exhibition held at the
Seattle Art Museum in 1983 spotlighting the functional arts
of Japan. Everyday articles such as clothing, kitchen
utensils, and houseware, made by anonymous artisans for use
by common people are shown. The photographs are mostly in
black and white but are quite clear; they are accompanied by
information on origin, use, and significance of the articles
pictured. Bibliography.

1-023.   Sakade, Florence and Sono, Kazuhiko. Fold-and-Paste: Origami
Storybook. Rutland, VT: Tuttle, c. 1964. 31 p. (K-2)

Similar to Sakade's Origami: Japanese Paper Folding Play
(Rutland, VT: Tuttle, 1960), this book uses finished origami
foldings to illustrate five stories, two of which are
Japanese folktales. The stories are written in readable
English, and the background drawings have specified spaces
for mounting finished foldings. Although some of the
foldings are too complicated for the intended audience of
this book, some simple ones are also included. Paper for
making the origami is included.

1-024.   Sakade, Florence. Origami: Japanese Paper-Folding. Rutland,
VT: Tuttle, c. 1957-1959. 3 v. (K-6)

The art of Japanese paper folding, <u>origami</u>, is presented in
these three inexpensive paperbacks with easy-to-follow
instructions. The forty-eight figures introduced include
animals, birds, dolls, fish, flowers, boats, caps, boxes,
clowns, a clock, a jet plane, a space ship, a table and
chair, a tent, a house, a church, a windmill, a Christmas
tree, a lantern, Santa Claus, a fan, and a <u>kimono</u>. Besides
detailed diagrams for making each figure, the book also
includes suggestions for using the <u>origami</u> in finger plays,
party decorations, boat races, mobiles, space travel, and
hunting games.

1-025.   ------------. <u>Origami Storybook: Japanese Paper-Folding
          Play</u>. Illustrated by Kazuhiko Sono. Rutland, VT: Tuttle,
          1960. 31 p. (K-2)

This book uses the <u>origami</u> to illustrate scenes in stories
familiar to the children. Stories are retold in very brief
form. A completed paper folding is pasted in the book for
each story and all of them are easy for primary graders to
make. This book is suitable for an art class, and the
teacher can give meaning to the paper foldings by telling
the story.

1-026.   Sarasas, Claude. <u>The ABC's of Origami: Paper Folding for
          Children</u>. Illustrated by the author. Rutland, VT: Tuttle,
          c. 1964. 55 p. (K-4)

This book is arranged in the format of an alphabet book, and
under each letter of the alphabet, the construction of a
paper folding of something which begins with that letter is
illustrated with good, clear step-by-step diagrams. A
drawing ilustrates the setting for each finished paper
folding. This may encourage children to use their
imagination to draw their own settings for their paper
foldings. One third of the paper foldings in this book
requires less than seven steps and are simple enough for
younger children. The book has trilingual captions in
English, French, and romanized Japanese. Words for the
foldings are also given in Japanese characters.

1-027.   Soleillant, Claude. <u>Japan: Activities & Projects in Color</u>.
          New York: Sterling, c. 1980. 96 p. (3-9)

Originally published in French in 1977, this book includes
many ideas for celebrating Japanese festivals--costumes,
crafts, decorations, food, games, flower arrangements and a
story to read or act. All the crafts and the games are good.
Some of the illustrations of <u>kimono</u> are not correct, but the
pattern for the <u>kimono</u> is authentic. Several words are
misspelled: p. 6 <u>huia</u> should be <u>hina</u>, p. 7 <u>futus</u> should be

futon, kuydo should be kyudo, p. 38 mukado should be mukade, p. 48 matsy should be matsu, and sorii should be zori. The personal names of the characters in the story are not authentic.

1-028.   Spencer, Cornelia. Made in Japan. Borzoi Books. Illustrated by Richard Powers and with photographs. New York: Knopf, 1963. 210 p. (6-9)

The first chapter provides a brief history of Japan. The following chapters survey various forms of Japanese arts and crafts, such as the tea ceremony, gardens, painting, drama, music, and literature. An informative and useful book. Bibliography and index are included.

1-029.   Statler, Oliver. Modern Japanese Prints: An Art Reborn. Rutland, VT: Tuttle, c. 1959, 1967 printing. xxi, 209 p. (10 up)

A collection of woodblock prints by twenty-six artists active at the time of publication. This work picks up where Michener's Japanese Prints (see above) leaves off. There is an explanation for each print and information on the artist and his work. Abundantly illustrated by prints, mostly black and white. Appended with a list of woods used for making prints. Detailed index.

1-030.   Streeter, Tal. The Art of the Japanese Kite. New York: Weatherhill, 1974. 181 p. (6 up)

This is not only an "all about kites" book by an American sculptor who is "crazy about kites", it is also a wonderful book about Japan. The author visited many famous kite makers and kite festivals all over Japan and the descriptions and interviews in the text benefit from his trained artist's eye. The text includes a brief history of Oriental kites and directions on how to make and fly kites as well. Illustrated by one hundred and thirty pictures, many in color. The author's love for kites is contagious and makes the book interesting to readers, kite lovers or not. Appended with a fairly extensive reading list.

1-031.   Stevenson, John. Yoshitoshi's Thirty-Six Ghosts. New York: Weatherhill, 1983. 96 p. (5 up)

These full-page color prints depict scenes from traditional Japanese stories which contain elements of the supernatural. In Japanese, the word "ghost" includes spirits, monstrous beings, and ogres. The prints are imaginative, not sensational, and bring the old stories, retold on the page

opposite the print, back to life. There is a good
introduction on the idea of the Japanese ghost and detailed
notes on the artist and the drawings.

1-032.   Toba Sojo. Animal Frolic. Text by Verlma Vermer. New York:
Putnum, c. 1954 and 1967. Unpaged. (K-2)

This book is a reproduction of a scroll, known as Choju Giga
(Comical drawings of birds and animals), drawn by a Japanese
priest in the 12th century. This famous masterpiece is done
in black ink line drawings without the technique of
blurring. Lively caricatures of common animals are
entertaining and will stir children's imaginations. The text
was added to keep the flow of the story.

2. DRAMA

2-001.   Cocagnac, A.M. <u>The Three Trees of the Samurai</u>. Illustrated
          by Alain de Foll. New York: Harlin Quist, distributed by
          Dell, 1970. Unpaged. (2-6)

          An adaptation of a Japanese <u>No</u> play called "Hachi no Ki"
          (Trees in a Pot), based on a famous legend of a faithful
          <u>samurai</u> is almost a straight translation except that it is
          in story form. It is a typical Japanese story of loyalty to
          one's master. The text is in the classical style and well
          written. Some illustrations are inaccurate, for example, the
          woman's <u>kimono</u> is drawn as a bathrobe with a huge, strange
          sash, and the fireplace is not Japanese. This could easily
          be transformed into a play for the upper grades of
          elementary school.

2-002.   <u>Japanese folk-plays: The Ink-Smeared Lady and Other Kyogen</u>.
          Translated by Shio Sakanishi with illustrations by Yoshie
          Noguchi. Rutland, VT: Tuttle, c. 1960. xiii, 150 p. (7 up)

          Shio Sakanishi, who was a librarian at the Library of
          Congress, first published this collection of twenty-two
          <u>kyogen</u> in 1938. <u>Kyogen</u>, one of the lesser known Japanese
          drama forms, are short humorous plays generally performed
          between the acts of a <u>No</u> drama. They are folk plays which
          have been handed down orally and portray the less complex
          emotions and everyday experiences of simple personalities.
          They are normally short and easy to understand and would be
          easy to stage. There is an excellent introduction on the
          origin, history, authorship, and aesthetic value of <u>kyogen</u>
          and a select bibliography and list of translated <u>kyogen</u>.
          Includes black-and-white illustrations and a plan of a
          <u>kyogen</u> stage.

2-003.   Nippon Gakujutsu Shinkokai (The Japan Society for the
          Promotion of Science). Japanese Classics Translation
          Committee. The Special Noh Committee. The Noh Drama: Ten
          Plays from the Japanese. UNESCO Collection of
          Representative Works: Japanese Series. Rutland, VT:
          Tuttle, c. 1955, 1969 printing. xvi, 192 p. (10 up)

          Ten well-known No plays were selected and translated by
          specialists on the basis of the plays' appeal to the Western
          reader and their historical significance. Each play is
          preceded by an excellent introduction. The book is
          illustrated with good drawings; a plan of a No stage, a map,
          and an index are also included. These plays could be used
          for dramatic presentation as well as read as literature.

2-004.   Takeda, Izumo, Miyoshi, Shoraku, and Namiki, Senryu.
          Chushingura: The Treasury of Loyal Retainers: A Puppet
          Play. Translated by Donald Keene. New York: Columbia
          University Press, c. 1971. 183 p. (10 up)

          Donald Keene presents a complete translation of the original
          text of the puppet play about the historical Ako vendetta.
          He provides extensive notes and an excellent, detailed
          introduction. The play consists of eleven short acts and
          tells how the ronin, or masterless samurai, avenged their
          lord's enemy. Appended with a list of works consulted.
          Chushingura, also known as the story of Forty-Seven Ronin,
          is the most famous and popular Japanese drama.

2-005.   Waley, Arthur. The No Plays of Japan. New York: Grove Press,
          c. 1957. 319 p. (10 up)

          Originally published in 1920. Inludes nineteen No plays, a
          kyogen (a No farce), summaries of sixteen other No plays,
          and an extensive introduction to No drama. Waley, a well-
          known scholar of Japanese and Chinese literature, added
          notes for each of the plays. There is an index and plans for
          a No play. Several plays could be performed by high school
          students.

3. MUSIC

3-001.   Berger, Donald Paul. Folk Songs of Japanese Children.
         Compiled, arranged, and annotated. Illustrated by Yoshie
         Noguchi. Rutland, VT: Tuttle, c. 1969. 63 p. (K-6)

         Excellent selection of fifteen simple traditional Japanese
         children's songs with piano accompaniment. Includes notes on
         pronunciation, and each of the fifteen songs has a good
         introduction and a literal translation as well as verses
         both in English and in Japanese. If the song is accompanied
         with games or movements, these are also explained. Good
         authentic illustrations. Highly recommended for music class
         and social studies.

3-002.   Dietz, Betty, and Park, Thomas Choonbai. Folk Songs of
         China, Japan, Korea. New York: Day, 1964. 47 p. (K-6)

         A get-acquainted songbook for young children. Includes a
         note to teachers on pronunciation and gives more songbooks
         and record references. Musical notes for the piano
         accompaniment and English translations are given for each
         song along with lyrics in the Oriental language. A brief
         introduction is also given for the first verse of each song.
         Accompanied by a good phono-disc. Most selections are not
         particularly suitable for children, although some are easy
         enough for young children to sing in the classroom.

3-003.   Hattori, Ryotaro. Japanese Folk-Songs. 4th ed. Tokyo: The
         Japan Times, 1960, 88 p. (4 up)

         A collection of thirty-three representative Japanese folk
         songs. All the songs have simple melodies and rhythms, and
         for each song, the piano accompaniment is given. The verse
         is provided in both Japanese (syllabary and romanization)
         and English. There is an explanatory note for each song.
         Includes some black-and-white illustrations.

3-004.   Hirawa. Yasuko. <u>Song of the Sour Plum and Other Japanese</u>
          <u>Children's Songs</u>. Translated by Y. Hirawa. Illustrated by
          Setsuko Majima. New York: Walker, c. 1968. Unpaged. (K-3)

          Good translation of Japanese nursery rhymes and old poems
          with clear, bright, and lively illustrations. Not all the
          poems and rhymes are particularly typical of Japanese
          Children's songs, but this is a good addition to the body of
          Japanese children's songs in English. Especially good for
          younger children.

3-005.   <u>101 Favorite Songs Taught in Japanese Schools</u>. Essays and
          translations by Ichiro Nakano. Illustrations by Sachiko
          Higuchi. Tokyo: The Japan Times, c. 1983. x, 274 p. (K-12)

          This bilingual collection is compiled to introduce well-
          known songs, most of them children's songs, to those
          interested in Japan and Japanese culture. The songs are
          grouped in four categories: old airs of Japan; <u>warabe uta</u>
          (nursery songs); songs influenced by Western music; and
          songs by Japan's own modern poets. Piano accompaniment,
          Japanese and English verse, notes about the song, and an
          illustration accompany each song. A short essay on the
          development of music education in Japanese schools is
          included.

3-006.   White, Florence, and Akiyama, Kazuo. <u>Children's Songs from</u>
          <u>Japan</u>. Illustrated by Toshihiko Suzuki. New York: Marks
          Music Corp., c. 1960. 92 p. (K-6)

          An outstanding collection of popular Japanese children's
          songs on the bilingual principle, with very clear
          illustrations. Translations are excellent. This book teaches
          both musical and social aspects of Japanese culture. Divided
          into five sections: Creatures large and small; singing
          games; singing day by day; seasons and festivals; and street
          cries. Often explanations of the games and customs are
          given. Excellent book for classroom use. Includes index.

4. FICTION

4-001.   Allyn, John. <u>The Forty-Seven Ronin Story</u>. Rutland, VT:
          Tuttle, c. 1970. 240 p. (9 up)

This exciting story is an account of a historical event
which took place in 1702. In a moment of anger and
frustration, Lord Asano drew his sword in the Shogun's
castle and injured a corrupt official. Since merely to draw
a sword within the castle grounds was a crime punishable by
death, Lord Asano was ordered to commit <u>seppuku</u> (<u>hara-kiri</u>
or disembowelment). His fief was confiscated and his
retainers became masterless <u>samurai</u> or <u>ronin</u>. Forty-seven of
Lord Asano's faithful retainers vowed to avenge their lord's
death by killing the corrupt official whose words had caused
their master to commit the deed punishable by death. The
<u>ronin</u> waited patiently for two years until an opportunity
presented itself. Their success satisfied the ethical
demands of <u>samurai</u> philosophy but ran them afoul of the need
for an orderly society and they, like their master before
them, were required to commit <u>seppuku</u>. Their act of loyalty
to their master made them heroes and has been celebrated
throughout history in songs, stories, plays, and now in
movies. Very well written and a good introduction to <u>samurai</u>
mentality.

4-002.   Ariyoshi, Sawako. <u>The Doctor's Wife</u>. Translated by Wakako
          Hironaka and Ann Siller Kosatant. New York: Kodansha
          International, c. 1978. viii, 174 p. (9 up)

This fascinating story is based on the life of Seishu
Hanaoka, a Japanese doctor who lived from 1760 to 1845 and
who succeeded in making general anesthesia from herbal
medicine. Behind his success were sacrifices by his mother,
wife, and sisters. Seishu's ambition propels the women in
his life, his mother, Otsugi, and his wife, Kae, into
constant conflict. The beautiful, clever, assertive Otsugi

is responsible for the prosperity of the Hanaoka family.
Through her initiative, her son studies medicine in Kyoto,
and in typical Japanese manner, she finds him a wife. A
daughter-in-law was chosen on the basis of her projected
worth as a laborer, a child-bearing machine, and as an
assistant for her husband. Conflict between mother-in-law
and daughter-in-law was typical of the family system in
Japan. This story could be used for the study of family
and/or women in Japan.

4-003.   Bannon, Laura. The Other Side of the World. Written and
          illustrated by Laura Bannon. Boston: Houghton Mifflin, c.
          1960. 48 p. (K-2)

The author of this book has a unique and well-calculated
approach to make younger children understand differences in
customs and also that all human beings live under one sun.
Sometimes the illustrations depict outmoded and inaccurate
clothing and customs such as having all the storekeepers
hold fans. Drawings also mix seasons: one, for example,
shows a rice planting scene, which takes place in June, in
conjunction with watermelons which come out in late summer.

4-004.   Baruch, Dorothy W. Kappa's Tug-of-War with Big Brown Horse:
          The Story of a Japanese Water Imp. With paintings by
          Sanryo Sakai. Rutland, VT.: Tuttle, 1962. 36 p. (K-3)

Kappa, a mythical creature who lives in the river, tries to
steal a farmer's horse. The farmer and the Kappa have a
tug-of-war, and the farmer wins and gets the horse back, but
he is kind enough to spare the kappa's life. The grateful
kappa brings presents to the farmer ever afterward.
Illustrations done by a Japanese artist in the traditional
painting style, using misty watercolors. This book could
pass for an art book. A lively, amusing, and pleasant story.

4-005.   ----------------. Kobo and the Wishing Picture: A Story from
          Japan. Illustrated by Yoshie Noguchi. Rutland, VT: Tuttle,
          c. 1964. 63 p. (1-4)

Kobo, a Japanese boy, want to combine becoming strong,
brave, and lucky in one wish for Wishing Day. He decides to
draw a horse by himself to show his wish because his artist
father is too busy drawing pictures for Wishing Day for his
customers. Although a Japanese custom is explained in an
interesting way with very good illustrations, the text has
some jumbled, stereo-typed expressions, such as "Honorable
artist," "Honorable husband," "Come, elder son," and there
are some mistakes in word usage, such as the word "Hai"
meaning yes.

4-006.   Battles, Edith. What does the Rooster Say, Yoshio? Pictures
          by Toni Hormann. Chicago: Whitman, c. 1978. 32 p. (K-1)

          A Japanese boy meets an American child in a play farm. Each
          child says in his own language the cry or sound the
          different animals make. They are all different except for
          the cow and in both languages the sound is "Moo." This story
          allows very young children to understand the difference in
          languages and at the same time lets them find something in
          common.

4-007.   Breck, Vivian. The Two Worlds of Noriko. Garden: N.Y.:
          Doubleday, c. 1966. 190 p. (7-12)

          The story of a second generation Japanese-American girl who
          is taken to Japan by her parents as a college graduation
          gift. While in Japan, her parents push her to marry a
          relative, a young Japanese farmer who lives in an isolated
          village. Aware of the tremendous gap between her background
          and his, she decides to return to the United States. The
          book contains much information about the culture, customs,
          and philosophy of the Japanese.

4-008.   Buck, Pearl. The Big Wave. Illustrated with prints by
          Hiroshige and Hokusai. New York: Day, originally published
          in 1947, reprinted in 1973. 61 p. (4-6)

          This is a story of a Japanese boy in a fishing village, and
          how he grows into manhood. Jiya's family and his home are
          lost in a tidal wave, but he survives because he escaped to
          his friend's house on the hillside. The names Jiya and Kino
          are neither Japanese boys' first names nor last names.
          Descriptions of the Japanese countryside are vague and
          obscure. Not particularly good.

4-009.   Bunting, Eve. Magic and the Night River. Illustrated by Say
          Allen. New York: Harper & Row, c. 1978. 44 p. (3-6)

          This is a heart-warming story about the strong tie between a
          boy and his grandfather and their cormorants, which are
          fishing birds. Authentic, very attractive illustrations by
          the author/illustrator of Once Upon the Cherry Blossom Tree
          and The Feast of Lanterns. A little strong on morality.

4-010.   Carlson, Dade. Warlord of the Genji. Illustrated by John
          Gretzer. New York: Atheneum, 1970. 171 p. (5 up)

          Historical tale of how Yoshitsune, the young warlord of the
          Genji, an outlawed clan, accomplished the seemingly
          impossible task of leading his clan to victory against a
          posperous rival clan, the Heike, to help his elder brother,
          Yoritomo. Yoshitsune and his men and family suffer and die
          tragic deaths because of Yoritomo's envy of the popularity

and fame which Yoshitsune gains. Yoshitsune was a real
person, and his life story is based on good historical
evidence and on legend. Well-told, historically accurate,
and detailed; an exciting story of twelfth century Japan.
Illustrations are well done. Highly recommended for
individual reading.

4-011.   Clavell, James. Shogun. New York: Dell, 1975. 1210 p. (10
          up)

Many students have been introduced to this novel through the
television movie. It is the fast-moving, dramatic biography
of an English boat pilot, Will Adams, who spent many years
in the emply of Japanese lords. The novel is an interesting
introduction to seventeenth-century Japan.

4-012.   Coatsworth, Elizabeth. The Cat Who Went to Heaven.
          Illustrated by Lynd Ward. New York: Macmillan, reprinted
          in 1967. 62 p. (3-6)

Based on the legend that the cat, being a sly animal, was
not included in Buddha's nirvana. Told in an old style (this
book was originally published in 1931), but the author has a
good grasp of what Buddha's mercy is like. The text contains
some strictly literal translations, but the book still has a
place in modern classrooms.

4-013.   ---------------. Cricket and the Emperor's Son. Drawings by
          Juliette Palmer. New York: Norton, c. 1962. 126 p. (3-6)

Japanese version of Arabian Nights. A Japanese boy nicknamed
Cricket who is an apprentice of a merchant learns that the
emperor's son is incurably ill. He goes to the palace to
visit the prince and reads from a magic paper he found on
the street. There are several textual as well as
illustrative mistakes. For example, there are no water
buffalo in Japan, and chairs were not used in traditional
Japan. Some of the names in the story are Chinese and some
are Japanese. The illustrator ignored historical evidence;
for example, the cover depicts two boys with girls' clothing
and modern boys' hairdos and a lady-in-waiting with a man's
hairdo. Although this author has a big name in children's
literature, this work is not recommended.

4-014.   Collins, David. Kim Soo and His Tortoise. Illustrated by
          Alix Cohen. New York: The Lion Press, c. 1970. 48 p. (K-3)

This is classified in the sources as a Japanese story only
because the author claims that it is Japanese. The name Kim
Soo is Korean. It is difficult to identify nationality from
the illustrations of this book since illustrations mix
customs of many places.

4-015.   Contemporary Japanese Literature: An Anthology of Fiction,
          Film, and Other Writing Since 1945. New York: Knopf, 1977.
          xiv, 468 p. (9 up)

          This anthology is a collection of works which have not
          previously been translated into English. It includes fiction
          as well as plays, film scripts, and poems. Although some of
          the works might not be suitable for high school students,
          many are.

4-016.   Damjan, Miacha. The Little Prince and the Tiger Cat.
          Illustrated by Ralph Steadman. New York: McGraw-Hill, c.
          1967. Unpaged. (K-2)

          An emperor of Japan who reigned in an age when people
          believed that cats were sorcerers issues a leashing law for
          cats. Later he changes his mind because he finally realizes
          that cats catch mice. There are many textual and factual
          mistakes; neither the author nor the illustrator apparently
          had any intention of maintaining authenticity. The author
          sets the stage for this story in Japan, I suspect, simply
          to make it exotic. Illustrations are half Chinese, half
          Western with a touch of Japanese. Do not use.

4-017.   Fifield, Flora. Pictures for the Palace. Pictures by Nola
          Langer. New York: Vanguard Press, c. 1957. Unpaged. (K-3)

          The story was based on the legends concerning the life of
          Hokusai, a famous Japanese artist, who was born more than
          two hundred years ago. It is an exciting, interesting story
          and the illustrations are lively and attractive, but some of
          the details in both the story and illustrations are
          incorrect.

4-018.   Floethe, Louise Lee. A Thousand and One Buddhas. Illustrated
          by Richard Floethe. New York: Farrar, c. 1967. Unpaged.
          (K-4)

          Many years ago there lived an emperor of Japan named
          Goshirakawa. He ordered a beautiful temple with 1001 Buddha
          statues to be built in Kyoto, the ancient capital, with the
          hope of inspiring his people to live in spiritual peace. The
          temple and the Buddha statues can still be seen today. Both
          author and illustrator paid close attention to historical
          evidence for settings, customs, and clothing of twelfth
          century Japan. This could also be used in social studies.

4-019.   Flory, Jane. One Hundred and Eight Bells. Boston: Houghton
          Mifflin, c. 1963. 219 p. (3-6)

Very good dtailed description of the average Japanese
family. The daily life of the Japanese and the way the
Japanese think and act are vividly and accurately described.
Careless Setsuko, the twelve-year-old heroine, comes alive;
girls can easily identify with her. Jumbled literary
translations such as "honorably return," are to be
regretted, especially because the rest of the book is
outstanding. There is only one small mistake in the text,
where an illustration shows an old man in Japanese <u>kimono,</u>
the text says, "...handed the shoehorn." Japanese never wear
shoes with <u>kimonos</u>. Could also be used in social studies.

4-020.   Fortune, J.J. <u>Duel for the Samurai Sword</u>. Race Against Time.
          Laurel-Leaf Library. New York: Dell, c. 1984. 142 p. (5-9)

Stephen's parents go on a short vacation and leave Stephen
in Uncle Richard's care. Uncle Richard receives a request
from Master Ohara, his former martial arts master, to come
to Tokyo immediately. Stephen and Uncle Richard fly to
Japan, and Master Ohara who is close to death gives Uncle
Richard a sword made by Masamune, the most famous swordmaker
who ever lived in Japan. Another former pupil of Master
Ohara who had become a <u>yakuza</u>, a gangster, also wants the
sword. Uncle Richard, Stephen, and the dead master's
daughter, Aka, have many dangerous encounters in Tokyo while
protecting the sword, and the two Americans still manage to
return home before Stephen's parents come back from
vacation. Not a very realistic story, but it is exciting and
the descriptions of modern Tokyo are accurate,. as are the
many Japanese words and sentences included. Illustrated.

4-021.   Gallant, Kathryn. <u>The Flute Player of Beppu</u>. Illustrated by
          Kurn Wiese. New York: Coward, 1960. 44 p. (K-3)

Everyone in Beppu, Japan, loved the flute player, but no one
loved him so much as the young boy, Sato. One day, Sato
found the flute which the flute player had dropped, and
after overcoming the temptation to keep it, returned it. The
flute player in return, taught the boy how to play the
flute, and after years of practice, the boy himself became
the flute player of Beppu. The hero of the story, a little
Japanese boy, is called Sato-San all the way through the
book. Sato is either a last name or a girls first name. In
addition, little boys are not called San in this context.
The author has the stereo-typed idea that Japanese always
address people by their last name with honorific "san." This
idea is also shown when the flute player's wife calls her
husband by saying, "Come, Flute-player-san." The phrase "Ah,
so" is also wrongly used. Illustrations are not authentic.

4-022.   Garrison, Christian. <u>The Dream Eater</u>. Pictures by Diane
          Goode. Scarsdale, NY: Bradbury Press, c. 1978. 32 p. (1-3)

A <u>baku</u>, a mythical animal which lives on bad dreams, is saved from dying of hunger by Yukio, a young Japanese boy, while the villagers are left to enjoy peaceful and undisturbed sleep. The story is fine; but the illustrations, which by themselves are beautifully done, are a mixture of Chinese and Japanese elements, which detracts from the book.

4-023.   Gray, Elizabeth. <u>The Cheerful Heart</u>. New York: Viking, c. 1959. 176 p. (4-6)

Good, realistic story of a family with an eleven-year-old girl with a cheerful heart who brightens the world around her. The setting is Tokyo right after World War II. Vivid descriptions of how most Japanese lived during that period. Could also be used for social studies.

4-024.   Greekmore, Raymond. <u>Fujio</u>. Story and lithographs by Raymond Greekmore. New York: Macmillan, c. 1951. Unpaged. (1-5)

The story of Fujio, a country boy who wants to climb Mt. Fuji. There are mistakes both in the text and in the illustrations. The Dolls' Festival takes place in March instead of April as stated in the text. Country boys do not call their father "papa-san" (an English word with the honorific <u>san</u>), they use the Japanese word "otosan" (father). The clothing and illustrations of <u>hina</u> dolls for Dolls' Festival are not authentic.

4-025.   Guest, Lynn. <u>The Sword of Hachiman: A Novel of Early Japan</u>. New York: McGraw-Hill, 1981. 310 p. (9 up)

This historical novel of a colorful, romantic period centers on the heroic, but tragic, life of Minamoto no Yoshitsune, the younger brother of the first <u>shogun</u> in Japanese history. The power struggle between the emperor, the retired emperor, the nobility, and the newly arisen warrior class in the twelfth century is presented in an exciting story. Yoshitsune is a favorite Japanese tragic hero.

4-026.   Hall, Tom H. <u>Golden Tombo</u>. A Borzoi Book. Written and illustrated by Tom H. Hall. New York: Knopf, c. 1959. Unpaged. (K-3)

A story of a Japanese boy and his summer vacation. The school project for the summer is to collect insects. But all summer long, this boy has to help his father in the field and worries about not finishing the project. But on the last day of summer vacation, he catches a huge dragonfly. Both text and illustrations are accurate except for a few flaws. Teachers do not wear <u>kimonos</u> with the special hairdos and

fans to class; the illustration of the school entrance
actually depicts the entrance of a regular home; and
scarecrows are not needed for young rice fields.

4-027.   Hamada, Hirosuke. The Dragon's Tears: Picture Play for
          Kindergarten, School, and Home. Illustrated by Nao Kojima.
          Rutland, VT: Tuttle, c. 1964. 16 panels. (K-2)

The picture-play format, known in Japan as kamishibai which
literally means "paper play," is effectively used for
Hamada's The Tears of the Dragon. The text is simplified for
English translation, but there is no unnecessary change from
the original story. The excellent illustrations contribute
much to the text. Picture plays were very popular in Japan
among children. The children who buy candies from him are
allowed to watch the play and listen to his stage elocution.
Highly recommended for classroom use.

4-028.   ---------------. The Tears of the Dragon. Illustrated by
          Chihiro Iwasaki, English version by Alvin Tresselt. New
          York: Parents' Magazine, c. 1967. Unpaged. (K-3)

This story is always listed as a story of Japan in reference
sources because the translator added the line "Once in the
far land of Japan," It was only written by a Japanese
author; the setting of the story was not Japan. The author
specifies the stage of the story as "a far-away country in
the south." All the illustrations in this particular book
are in authentic Chinese style. The boy is also given a
Japanese name, although in the original text he has no name.
Misleading, but the story itself is a good one and teaches
the value of kindness.

4-029.   Hart, Laverne. You May Wear Your Shoes in Church.
          Illustrated by Paul R. Behrens. Nashville, TN: [s.n.], c.
          1981. 32 p. (K-4)

Story of an American missionary family in Japan. The story
relates how the children learned to understand this new and
different culture. A nice story that is realistic and
interesting.

4-030.   Haugaard, Erik Christian. The Samurai's Tale. Boston:
          Houghton Mifflin, 1984. xiv, 234 p. (5-9)

This novel is based on research done by the author on the
Takeda family, an important warrior family of the sixteenth
century. (The movie Kagemusha is also about this family.) A
young samurai was killed in a battle against the Takeda, and
following the practice of the time, his wife and older
children were also killed to prevent the family from trying
to avenge the warrior's death. The youngest son was spared,

and the story tells of the boy's struggles to become a
samurai. After many hardships and exciting experiences, the
young man becomes a member of a feudal lord's warrior band.
When his lord is killed in battle, the samurai decided not
to avenge his master's death, as was expected of all
samurai, but to live in peace with his beloved wife.
Accurate, well-told tale with a clear message.

4-031.   Heller, George. Hiroshi's Wonderful Kite. Our World of
People Series: Japan. Illustrated by Kyuzo Tsugami.
Morristown, NJ: Silver, 1968. 32 p. (1-4)

Hiroshi is doing an important errand for his father by
delivering a bolt of silken cloth to one of his father's
customers. He is robbed, but he flies a kite from the top of
the pickup truck to signal his friend, Tsuyoshi, to find
help. Good material to use for introducing the Japanese
life. Illustrations are very clear and good. Includes a
glossary of Japanese words.

4-032.   Hirsh, Marilyn. How the World Got Its Color. New York:
Crown, c. 1972. 32 p. (K-2)

This is an interesting story which is supposed to have been
adapted from the Japanese. But the only thing which is
really Japanese is the little girl's name. Illustrations,
done by the author, try to look Japanese, but they are not
authentic.

4-033.   Hope, Laura Lee. The Bobbsey Twins and the Goldfish Mystery.
New York: Grosset, c. 1962. 175 p. (3-6)

The Bobbsey twins go to Japan with their family and solve
two mysteries there. Descriptions of Japanese culture are
accurate and Japanese words are accurately used but the
details of the illustrations are sometimes inaccurate.

4-034.   Ihara, Saikaku. Tales of Samurai Honor. A Monumenta
Nipponica Monograph; 57. Translated by Caryl Ann Callahan.
Tokyo: Monumenta Nipponica. Sophia University, c. 1981.
156 p. (9 up)

Buke Giri Monogatari, the original of this translation, was
first published in 1688, when the samurai class was the
social and political elite. In the introduction, the
translator describes the society and period in which Saikaku
was writing as well as discusses the implications of
samurai's concept of honor or giri. Saikaku writes with
irony and vividness and is a very good story teller.
Illustrated with the wood-block prints which appeared in the
original. Includes a bibliography and an index.

4-035.   Inui, Tomiko. Village of Snowy Herons. Japanese Children's
          Books: 1. Translated by Shigeo Watanabe. Illustrated by
          Kazuho Hieda. Tokyo: Uchida Rokakuho Publishing, 1959.
          Unpaged. (K-2)

          The story of a friendship between Taro, his friend Mitsuko,
          and a snowy heron which fell out of its nest during a storm.
          The children take care of the injured bird, and after its
          wound is healed, the heron leaves this Japanese village to
          migrate south. Beautiful, watercolor illustrations. Not
          particularly Japanese, but the story is staged in a small
          village in northern Japan.

4-036.   Ishii, Momoko. The Dolls' Day for Yoshiko. Translated by
          Yone Mizuta. Illustrated by Mamoru Funai. Chicago:
          Follett, 1966. 94 p. (3-5)

          Yoshiko, a ten-year-old Japanese girl never owned a set of
          royal dolls for Dolls' Festival, held each year on the third
          of March. Her mother owned a very beautiful set when she was
          a girl, so she is determined that Yoshiko should own a set
          as nice as the one she once had. Because Yoshiko's father
          had passed away a few years earlier, it is difficult for the
          family to afford a nice set. Yoshiko and her mother go to
          look for a set but they cannot find one they both like.
          Finally, Yoshiko's mother comes up with a wonderful solution
          which is more than satisfactory for both of them. A good,
          quiet story of warm feelings and understanding between a
          mother and a daughter.

4-037.   Kawaguchi, Sanae. Taro's Festival Day. Stories and pictures
          by the author. Boston: Little, Brown, c. 1957. 41 p. (K-2)

          Story of one Boys' Festival when Taro went dragonfly hunting
          with his friend. Information in the book is inaccurate and
          unreliable. For example, the season for dragonfly hunting is
          in late summer and the Boys' Festival is in early May. The
          children of present-day Japan do not wear kimonos to school
          or after school; in addition the kimonos in the
          illustrations resemble bathrobes. There is no such thing as
          "soy-bean noodles." Not recommended.

4-038.   Keene, Donald, ed. Anthology of Japanese Literature: From
          the Earliest Era to the Mid-Nineteenth Century. UNESCO
          Collection of Representative Works. New York: Grove Press,
          c. 1955. 442 p. (10 up)

          This well-known comprehensive collection of Japanese
          classical literature includes a great variety of literary
          forms, grouped into five historical periods. There is an
          excellent introduction by Keene, an internationally known
          scholar of Japanese literature. Most of the selections are

accompanied by introductory remarks and all are well
translated. The reader will gain "not only a picture of the
literature produced in Japan over the centuries, but an
understanding of the Japanese people as their lives and
aspirations have been reflected in their writings." A short
bibliography is included.

4-039.   Kirkup, James. Insect Summer. Woodcuts by Naoko Matsubara.
          New York: Knopf, c. 1971. 175 p. (5 up)

The story of three children during summer vacation on
Hajinoshima, a small remote Japanese island. A dry, hot,
uneventful summer quickly became exciting. Some new and
interesting people come to the island, the children find an
old sword, and the American pen pal of one of the children
writes that her family is coming to live in Japan for three
years. The author, a well-known English poet, lived in Japan
for years and in this story clearly evokes the heavy,
drowsy, heat of the Japanese summer. Very visual; a well-
written story.

4-040.   Kirn, Ann. Bamboo. Calligraphy by Satoru Takeuchi. New York:
          Putnam, c. 1966. 32 p. (K-1)

A story of how Bamboo, the monkey who lives in a Japanese
bamboo grove and likes the color orange, and acquires an
orange parasol. Illustrations are done in a mock-Japanese
sumi-e style and each illustration is accompanied with a
short phrase in Japanese writing. There is, however, no
romanization of the phrases nor translations, so the
calligraphy is useless except for giving a Japanese flavor.
Not a good book.

4-041.   Laurin, Anne. Perfect Crane. Illustrated by Charles
          Mikolaycak. New York: Harper & Row, c. 1981. 31 p. (2-4)

Gami (not an authentic Japanese name), a talented magician,
is very lonely because he has no friends. He never speaks to
townsfolk nor do they speak to him. Gami is very good with
his magic and can even breathe life into the things he makes
with paper. One day, he makes a perfect crane with folded
paper and gives life to it so that he will not be alone
anymore. Gami takes his crane with him everywhere he goes.
People start to talk to Gami, and they even start coming to
his house. When winter nears, the crane leaves to fly south
to join a flock. Gami, unhappy to be alone again, sadly lets
the crane go. After the crane leaves, the neighbors continue
coming to Gami's house beause friendships have been
established. When spring comes, the crane comes back to Gami
as it promised. Judging from the illustrations, the story is
set in feudal Japan.

4-042.   Lewis, Mildred. The Honorable Sword. Illustrated by Panos
          Ghikas. Boston: Houghton Mifflin, 1960. 179 p. (5 up)

          A quick-moving, well-told story of an orphan and his friend
          who are forced to escape from the burning castle of the
          boy's father, who is the Lord of Yori. After many hardships,
          they fulfill their pledge to take revenge on their enemy and
          get back the honorable sword of their ancestor. The only
          trouble with this book is that the Japanese language is used
          in a distorted way. For example, the honorific san is too
          often used in the wrong places. The boy's father and his
          wife address their son as Taro-chan, which is a modern way
          of addressing young children, and the son addresses his
          mother as "ofukuro," which, according to the author's
          explanation, is the affectionate name for mothers. In
          reality, it is never used for addressing one's mother
          directly; it is used only for referring to mothers. In this
          seventeenth century story all the farmers have last names,
          which was not true until 1870.

4-043.   Lifton, Betty Jean. The Cock and the Ghost Cat. Illustrated
          by Eiichi Mitsui. New York: Atheneum, 1965. 34 p. (2-4)

          This is based on a Japanese folktale called Cat and Pumpkin.
          Old Gembei, who lives with a faithful rooster in a small
          Japanese village, allows a little kitten to live in his
          home, not knowing that it will turn into a ghost cat at
          night. The rooster suspects the cat and tries to warn his
          master, but his master does not understand. With the help of
          a holy monk who understands animal language, old Gembei's
          life is saved. The faithful cock, relieved that his master
          will be safe, dies of exhaustion. The story reflects the
          traditional Japanese moral of loyalty to and sacrificial
          death for the master. Very good illustrations add to the
          effectiveness of the story.

4-044.   ----------------. Dwarf Pine Tree. Illustrated by Fuku Akino.
          New York: Atheneum, 1965. 34 p. (2-5)

          A small, forgotten pine tree becomes a "perfect dwarf pine"
          to cure an ailing princess. The tree endures terrible pain
          and dies for her sake. A beautiful story of devotion and
          sacrifice, which is very Japanese. The author absorbs
          Japanese folklore and creates original stories for children;
          most of her books are very good. The illustrations are
          beautiful. Tengu, a long-nosed mythical creature who lives
          in the mountains, appears in this story.

4-045.   ----------------. Joji and the Amanojaku. Illustrated by Fuku
          Akino. New York: Norton, c. 1965. Unpaged. (K-2)

The story of how Joji, the scarecrow, and his crow friends
help a lady scarecrow who is in trouble with Amanojaku, a
mischievous goblin who opposes whatever others say or do.
This is not among the author's best works; the plot is poor
and the whole story is rather artificial and boring.

4-046.   ----------------. Joji and the Dragon. Illustrated by Eiichi
          Mitsui. New York: William Morrow, c. 1957. Unpaged. (K-2)

Joji, the scarecrow does not scare anyone. He even has many
crow friends. Joji makes his crow friends promise to eat
worms and not rice, but the farmer does not trust either
Joji or the crows. He hires a dragon as a scarecrow and
retires Joji into the barn. Joji's crow friends have a plan
to scare the dragon away so that Joji will get his job as a
scarecrow back. Illustrated with black-and-white drawings,
some depicting Japanese scenery, homes, farms, and farmers.

4-047.   ----------------. Joji and the Fog. Illustrated by Eiichi
          Mitsui. New York: Morrow, c. 1959. Unpaged. (K-2)

One day a frightful fog floats over the farmyard and settles
in the farmer's bathtub, threatening to kill all the
farmer's rice plants. Joji, the farmer's scarecrow,
embarrassed by his inability to protect the rice plants,
wants to become a scarefog instead of a scarecrow. His crow
friends think up a plan to scare the fog away to help Joji
and save the rice crop. Light but good story, and children
will enjoy it. Good and humorous illustrations.

4-048.   ----------------. Kap and the Wicked Monkey. Illustrated by
          Eiichi Mitsui. New York: Norton, c. 1968. Unpaged. (K-2)

Kap, the prince of the kappa, is a typical kappa. He has a
hard shell on his back, webbed hands and feet, a face like a
monkey, and most important of all, a shallow bowl filled
with water on the top of his head. He is mischievous and
always thinking about tricks to play on others. Near the
river where the kappa lives, there is a tree where a wicked
monkey, Saru, lives. The monkey and Kap do not get along.
One day, when Kap's father becomes sick from too much
moonshine, Saru takes advantage of Kap's desire to see his
father get well, tricks him and almost kills him before Kap
is saved by a crane Kap had previously saved from Saru. This
modern story incorporates the traditional legendary
attributes of kappa: playing tricks, dancing by moonlight,
stealing cucumbers, enmity directed toward monkeys, and
losing power if the water is lost from the shallow bowl on
top of the head. Humorous black-and-white drawings.

4-049.   ----------------. Kap the Kappa. Illustrated by Eiichi
          Mitsui. New York: Morrow, 1960. Unpaged. (K-2)

A baby <u>kappa</u>, one of the mischievous Japanese mythical water imps with webbed feet, wanders out of his father's kingdom to the human world. He gets lost and is brought up by a family as one of its own sons. It is a warm story of rural Japan and its people accompanied by good black-and-white illustrations.

4-050.   ----------------. <u>Many Lives of Chio and Goro</u>. Illustrated by Yasuo Segawa. New York: Norton, c. 1968. Unpaged. (K-2)

Goro and his forgetful wife Chio promise that they will be foxes in their next life, but Chio forgets what she was supposed to be when she is about to die. There is nobody around to ask, since her husband Goro has died before her. Chio tries to think hard, but she still cannot remember, and thus it takes many lives until the couple are reunited in the same form. Entertaining. Reincarnation is a Buddhist idea common in Japan. Many deaths and reincarnations are treated in the book, but the illustrator created a way which is just right to demonstrate them so that the book is not gloomy.

4-051.   ----------------. <u>One-Legged Ghost</u>. Illustrated by Fuku Akino. New York: Atheneum, c. 1968. Unpaged. (K-3)

This story starts with a mysterious one-legged creature flying to a small village in Japan. Even the mayor of the village does not know what to make of it, so the villagers decide it is a god (there are eight million gods in Japan, anyway) and build a shrine for it. Later little Yoshi, who found the creature, uses the shrine for a shelter on a rainy day. A beautiful, luminous, watercolor illustration shows the Japanese countryside very well.

4-052.   ----------------. <u>The Rice-Cake Rabbit</u>. Illustrated by Eiichi Mitsui. New York: Norton, c. 1966. Unpaged. (2-4)

Based on the Japanese legend that there is a rabbit making rice-cakes on the moon. A rabbit who wants to become a soldier, but who is also a good rice-cake maker, wins a match after long and hard training by <u>tengu</u>, (mythical creatures). He is dispatched to the moon to govern it, and he makes rice-cakes there. One error: The <u>samurai</u> warriors laugh a woman's laugh in this book.

4-053.   ----------------. <u>Taka-Chan and I: A Dog's Journey to Japan</u>. <u>By Runcible as Told to Betty Jean Lifton</u>. Photographs by Eikoh Hosoe. New York: Norton, c. 1967. 63 p. (K-3)

A fantasy told by Runcible, a dog, to Betty Jean Lifton, about his trip through a long, dark, hole from a beach on Cape Cod to a lonely beach in Japan, a country on the opposite side of the earth. The dog meets a Japanese girl, Taka-Chan, who has been imprisoned by a fearful Black Dragon. The latter demands that he and the other dragons should get offerings from the fishermen as they used to do. Runcible promises the dragon that he will deliver the message to the fishermen, and the dragon orders the dog to find the most faithful person in Japan to free Taka-Chan from her captivity. The setting of this fantasy is contemporary Japan, and the book is illustrated with excellent photographs by a famous Japanese photographer.

4-054.   Lippit, Noriko Mizuta and Selden, Kyoko Iriye, eds. and trans. Stories by Contemporary Japanese Women Writers. New York: Sharpe, c. 1982. xxiii, 221 p. (10 up)

Twelve stories written between 1938 and 1977 by Japanese women are offered in this collection. The authors are well-known in Japan but little known in other countries. Some of the stories provide insight into Japanese society and psychology and could be useful for the study of Japan at the high school level. The introduction details the story of women authors in Japanese literary history. Detailed notes about the authors and the translators are included at the end of the volume.

4-055.   Luenn, Nancy. The Dragon Kite. Illustrated by Michael Hague. New York: Harcourt Brace Jovanovich Publishers, c. 1982. Unpaged. (3-6)

This story is based on one of the many famous robberies by a legendary thief of seventeenth-century Japan. Goemon Ishikawa was the Robin Hood of old Japan, stealing from the rich and giving to the poor. He decided to steal the golden dolphins from the roof of the castle held by the shogun's son. To do so, he needed to build a giant dragon kite, and thus he apprenticed himself to an old kitemaker for four years. When he became skilled, he made the dragon kite and, with the help of some friends, managed to steal some of the golden dolphins. Unfortunately, Goemon was caught by the authorities and he, his family, and the old kitemaker were sentenced to death. The dragon kite, because it had been so well made, in the meantime had come to life and was able to rescue the whole party as they were about to be killed. The illustrations are very detailed and attractive, but some are inaccurate. Generally a well-written story.

4-056.   McKim, Audrey. Aiko and Her Cousin Kenichi. Illustrated by Jim Walker. New York: Friendship Press, c. 1967. 126 p. (1-3)

A story of a poor Japanese Christian family which lost its
father. In spite of all the hardships, the family members
are rich in heart and live with courage. They have been
estranged from the father's relatives for many years, but
through some happenings they become close again. Tender
story.

4-057.   Martin, Patricia Miles. The Greedy One. Illustrated by Kazue
          Mizumura. Chicago: Rand McNally, c. 1960. Unpaged. (2-4)

This story of a boy's pet bird on the day before the Boy's
Festival when everyone in Japan celebrates with good food,
and cloth carp and streamers are used for decoration. There
are several textual errors. The author says the huge carp
are made of paper, but actually they are made of cloth. The
author also says water buffalo are cultivating the rice
paddy, but they are oxen. There are also jumbled literal
translations such as, "Welcome to our humble house." No
little girl would use such a language to her friend. She
would be most likely to say, "Irrashai," which simply means,
"welcome."

4-058.   ----------------. Kumi and the Pearl. Drawn by Tom Kamil. New
          York: Putnam, c. 1968. 47 p. (2-5)

Ten-year-old Kumi, the granddaughter of a pearl farmer in
Japan, secretly practices how to dive to surprise her
grandfather. She saves his life when he falls into the ocean
by accident. There are both textual and illustrative
mistakes. One typical example: the text reads, "Kumi
unwrapped the scarf that held Momo...Kumi wrapped Momo
against her back," and what the readers see as an
illustration is a picture of a baby strangely wrapped in a
huge scarf hanging from Kumi's back. Actually the scarf is a
sash used to tie a baby to the back and there is a proper
way of doing this. There is other evidence of the author's
stereotyped thinking.

4-059.   ----------------. Little Two and the Peach Tree. Illustrated
          by Joan Breg. New York: Atheneum, c. 1963. 39 p. (2-5)

People's names, clothing, buildings, hairdos, and objects
mentioned in the book are a mixture of Chinese and Japanese.
The author does not demonstrate any knowledge of what a
farmer's life was like in old Japan. A sheer absurdity. Not
recommended.

4-060.   ----------------. Suzu and the Bride Doll. Illustrated by
          Kazue Mizumura. Chicago: Rand McNally, c. 1960. Unpaged.
          (2-5)

A fantasy of a little Japanese girl. Story itself is all right, but there are some stereotyped ideas. Going shopping in a jinrikisha (rickshaw) in 1960 is far from reality. Also, the word for aunt is used to mean grandmother. The word for grandmother is obaasan, not obasan. Usable story.

4-061.   Matsubara, Hisako, Sumurai. Translated from the German by Ruth Hein. New York: Times Books, 1980. 218 p. (9 up)

The story starts around the year 1900. Nagayuki marries into a proud samurai class family to become the husband of their only daughter. He graduates from the best university in Japan with good job offers. But because of his stubborn father-in-law's pride, Nagayuki goes to the United States to become a success. After arriving in the United States, he goes through many unexpected hardships including poverty, loses his wife and family, and he is not even able to save enough money to come back to Japan. When he finally comes back to Japan after sixty years, he wears worn suits, carries five suitcases of old letters, photographs, and diaries. He comes home as a complete failure and a tired and exhausted man. Still his relatives who have gathered to welcome him do not realize what he has actually become. They try to guess what kind of good things he has in those suitcases. This is a new type of story telling what happens when the samurai spirit is applied in a superficial way. The title samurai here is used in a cynical way. A very probable and sad story, told by the granddaughter, of an obedient but indecisive and weak man who becomes a sacrifice to his father-in-law's false samurai spirit.

4-062.   Matsuno, Masako. Chie and the Sport's Day. Illustrated by Kazue Mizumura. Cleveland: World, 1965. Unpaged. (K-3)

Chie became lonesome after her brother Ichiro started school and did not want to play with her any longer. But one sports' day event helped her regain her brother's friendship. Ichiro was the slowest runner in the class, and he was depressed on sports' day when Mother and Chie came to school to watch the events. Chie helps him out of that depression. Universal problems and joys. American children will experience empathy with these children. Readable text and good illustrations.

4-063.   ----------------. A Pair of Red Clogs. Illustrated by Kazue Mizumura. Cleveland: World, c. 1960. Unpaged. (K-2)

A grandmother tells her little granddaughter about the time she ruined her new clogs while playing when she stepped into a puddle and dirtied the new clogs. The feelings of the

little girl are skillfully described, and life in Japan in
the grandmother's time is shown very well with clear
illustrations.

4-064.   ----------------. Taro and the Tofu. Illustrated by Kazue
            Mizumura. Cleveland: World, 1962. Unpaged. (K-3)

Taro is sent to buy tofu, soy-bean cake, by his mother and
is mistakenly given more change than he is entitled to. He
discovers this when he stops at a candy store on the way
home. The struggle between Taro's conscience and the
temptation to keep the extra change to buy candies is a
universal theme. Illustrations clearly show a typical
Japanese shopping area. A warmly told story with a good
universal moral.

4-065.   Miller, Elizabeth K. Seven Lucky Gods and Ken-Chan.
            Illustrated by Yasuo Kazama. Rutland, VT.: Tuttle, 1969.
            40 p. (2-4)

One day, Ken-Chan, a ten-year-old Japanese boy who is a poor
fisherman's son, finds a heavy wallet with an expensive
charm of the Seven Lucky Gods. He thinks about all the
things he could buy for himself and his family, but he is an
honest boy and decides to return the wallet and the charm to
the owner. While he is sleeping that night, the Seven Lucky
Gods make plans for the boy's future to reward his honesty.
Although the legend of the Seven Lucky Gods was brought to
Japan from China, it became a folk belief and many Japanese
still believe in it. The story of each god is explained
clearly and accurately. Clear black-and-white illustrations.
Strong message of the value of honesty along with the
meaning of the Seven Lucky Gods.

4-066.   Miyazawa, Kenji. Winds and Wildcat Places. Translated by
            John Bester. Illustrated by Rokuro Taniuchi. Palo Alto,
            CA: Kodansha International, c. 1967. 95 p. (3 up)

Kenji Miyazawa is an ever-popular author among children and
adults alike. His fantastic style and ideas are universal,
but he is sometimes very Japanese, and his work shows the
deep influence of Buddhism. Six short stories are included
in this little book, and all of them are excellent. The
illustrations by Rokuro Taniuchi match the story's style.
Highly recommended.

4-067.   ----------------. Winds from Afar. Translated by John Bester.
            Graphic art by Bernard Leach. Palo Alto, CA: Kodansha
            International, c. 1972. 164 p. (3 up)

This collection of the sixteen excellent stories of Miyazawa is a sequel to Winds and Wildcat Places. The author depicts in his stories the hills, valleys, plains, and winter storms of northern Japan, and the basic human themes which will appeal to children and adults alike on both sides of the Pacific. Illustrated by the works of Bernard Leach. Most highly recommended.

4-068.   Morris, Ivan. ed. Modern Japanese Stories: An Anthology. UNESCO Collection of Representative Works--Japanese Series. Rutland, VT: Tuttle, c. 1962, 1977 printing. 512 p. (10 up)

This anthology of modern Japanese literature is a sequel to Anthology of Japanese Literature (Ed. Donald Keene, c. 1955) and covers late nineteenth century to the mid-twentieth century. Twenty-five short stories by different authors are included in the excellent anthology, and many stories reflect the Japanese society of the period within which they were written. The editor, a well-known scholar of Japanese literature, has written an extensive introduction. For each author represented, a short biography is included. Each story is illustrated by a black-and-white woodcut print by Masakazu Kuwata.

4-069.   Muku, Hatoju. The Golden Footprints. Adapted by Taro Yashima. Cleveland: World, c. 1960. Unpaged. (3-6)

A touching story of love and devotion and loyalty among a captured baby fox, its parents, and a boy in a mountainous village in Japan. The boy secretly gives food to the baby fox for a long period of time. When the boy is buried in an avalanche, the parent foxes come and dig him out. Well-told story. The translation is very good. The illustrations by the translator match the heavy mood of the story.

4-070.   Mydans, Shelley. The Vermillion Bridge. New York: Doubleday, 1980. x, 369 p. (8-12)

Well-researched and documented book about the woman who twice became the reigning sovereign (empress) of Japan. The time was the eighth century when Japan, for the first time, was greatly influenced by the civilization of China. The cultural upheaval, the power struggles, and the love stories of the time are recounted. The book is so detailed that the main story tends to be buried in the documentation.

4-071.   Nakatani, Chiyoko. The Day Chiro Was Lost. Cleveland: World, c. 1969. 29 p. (K-2)

Translation of <u>Maigo no Chiro</u>. Chiro, a puppy that belongs
to a little Japanese boy, is riding on a pickup truck one
day. When the truck stops to let a pedestrian cross the
street, Chiro gets off the truck thinking that he is home.
Chiro is lost and the story tells of his adventures as he
finds his way home. This is a good story that is very
naturally told and has extremely clear illustrations. It is
a good book to introduce young children to the people,
stores, and streets of Japan.

4-072.   Namioka, Lensey. <u>The Samurai and the Long-Nosed Devils</u>. New
York: McKay, c. 1976, also as Dell Books, 1979. 153 p. (5
up)

This is one of a series of mystery/adventure stories about
two <u>ronin</u> (masterless <u>samurai</u>), Zenta and Matsuzo. Set in
sixteenth-century Japan, the stories provide an exciting
introduction to some aspects of <u>samurai</u> life and the honor
code of the warrior class. In this book, the young <u>ronin</u>
become bodyguards for Portuguese missionaries who were among
the first Europeans to reach Japan. The story explores the
opposition to foreigners felt by many high-ranking Japanese,
on the one hand, and the protection and patronage provided
by other influential Japanese, on the other. Historically
accurate. An exciting book.

4-073.   ----------------. <u>Valley of the Broken Cherry Trees</u>. New
York: Delacorte Press, c. 1980. 218 p. (5 up)

Zenta and Matsuzo come to rest one spring in a valley famous
for its beautiful cherry blossoms. Instead, they are
confronted with a series of events from the felling of old,
grand cherry trees to plots of assassination which require
their resourcefulness to handle. Suspenseful, exciting,
humorous story.

4-074.   ----------------. <u>Village of the Vampire Cat</u>. New York:
Delacorte Press, c. 1981. 200 p. (5-12)

Zenta and Matsuzo return to a village to celebrate New
Year's Day with Zenta's tea ceremony teacher. They find the
village and the tea master living in fear of a Vampire Cat
who attacks and kills young girls. The two <u>ronin</u> save the
master's niece from the Cat and find out who the Vampire Cat
is and what he was truly after. Exciting, well-written
story. Highly recommended.

4-075.   ----------------. <u>White Serpent Castle</u>. New York: McKay, c.
1976. 154 p. (5 up)

In this story, the two heroes of this mystery/adventure
series arrive at a castle where a succession dispute is
raging after the death of the feudal lord. The older son of
the dead lord was cast out of the castle ten years earlier,
but everyone expects him to return now that his father is
gone. The younger son, who is only nine years old and a
half-brother to the older son, is the designated heir
apparent. To further complicate matters, the lord's daughter
who is a full sister to the older son is determined to wait
for her brother's return. The night our two heroes arrive at
the castle, an envoy sent by the overlord to settle the
matter is killed and strange things take place. All the
parties want the warriors' help. When the fighting ends,
Zenta wants to leave even though he was offered a good
position in the household. Matsuzo learns that Zenta was the
long lost brother who had returned to help his sister and
half-brother in time of crisis. Like her other stories, this
is a very well-calculated, well-planned, well-researched
historical adventure story with excitement and humor. The
reader can learn about the honor code of warriors and the
life style of the samurai class. A list of characters who
appear in the story is given as well as a bibliography.
Highly recommended.

4-076.   Natsume, Soseki. Botchan. Translated by Umeji Sasaki.
Rutland, VT: Tuttle, c. 1968, 1980 printing. 188 p. (5 up)

Botchan was written in 1904 by a famous Japanese novelist.
This ever-popular, humorous, and warm story of a young man
who combined old idealism and a modern independent attitude
in his daring and non-conforming personality is recommended
for young readers. Botchan breezes through life from
catastrophe to catatrosphe, many resulting from his brutal
honesty. He alienates many people, including his family, but
retains the total loyalty and affection of his nursemaid no
matter what he does.

4-077.   Ness, Evaline. A Double Discovery. New York: Scribner, c.
1965. (K-3)

The setting of this story is Japan, but the story is a
completely fictional animal story of an old monkey named
Saru, a mustang named Hoki, and a little boy named Norio.
Not an exciting story, and although the stage is set in
Japan, neither the story nor illustrations have anything to
do with Japanese culture.

4-078.   Nikly, Michelle. The Emperor's Plum Tree. Translated from
the French by Elizabeth Shub. New York: Greenwillow Books,
1982. Unpaged. (K-3)

A nightingale, who is the friend of a little Japanese boy,
loses his home when the plum tree in which he nests is
chosen to replace a dead tree in the Emperor's perfect
garden. The Emperor realizes his selfishness thanks to the
brave little boy and makes the right decision. A short, but
good story of humanity and friendship. Each page of text is
accompanied by a full-page color illustration, most of which
are good.

4-079.   Nugent, Ruth. Our Japanese Playmates: The Adventures of Two
         American Children in Japan. Illustrated by Fusako Hyuga.
         Rutland, VT: Tuttle, 1960. 64 p. (2-4)

The author knows very well what interests children, and the
flow of the story ties everything in the book together.
Natural, detailed, clear, and informative. Written in big
type and in easy English so second and third graders can
read the book by themselves and enjoy it. Descriptive
illustrations help the children understand the story better.

4-080.   Ono, Chiyo. Which Way, Geta? Camden, NJ: Nelson, 1969. 26 p.
         (K-4)

Translation of Watashi no Geta (My Shoes). A Japanese girl
spends an evening chasing after her new wooden clogs and
kicking them ahead once she has retrieved them. The
repetition of these acts takes her through a variety of
Japanese streets and houses which are illustrated in
beautiful pastel color drawings.

4-081.   Ozawa, Ryokichi. Jingo. Plattsburgh, NY: Tundra Books, c.
         1977. 32 p. (K-2)

This is a translation of a Japanese story. Jingo, the best
cat carpenter in a Japanese town, likes to invent things.
One day, he receives an order to make a mouse trap. This is
a pocket-sized book with attractive illustrations.

4-082.   ----------------. Toko. Plattsburgh, NY: Tundra Books, c.
         1977. 32 p. (K-2)

This tiny book is about Toko, the cat barber, who treasures
his morning glory more than his work. Because of his lack of
enthusiasm for his work, his business is slow. But after
accidentally winning in a whiskers' competition, he starts
to enjoy a good business. Originally published by Fukuinkan
in Tokyo in 1975 under title: Tokomasa no Hanashi.

4-083.   Paterson, K. The Master Puppeteer. Illustrated by Haru
         Wells. New York: Crowell, c. 1975. 179 p. (5 up)

A breathtaking, quick-moving story of a brave, faithful, and
spirited thirteen-year-old boy who becomes an apprentice to
a puppeteers' group in Osaka in the feudal period when there
were famines year after year and chivalrous robbers were
prowling about the city. The author's effort in going to
Japan to ascertain the authenticity of her story and by
doing research on the puppets and puppeteers' lives is
repaid by the good work she produced. The atmosphere of the
period is well described and reproduced in this story,
although a few mistakes still remain. One which occurs
frequently is the way characters address one another. For
instance she lets the apprentices address their master as
"Yoshida," but apprentices would never address their masters
by the last name, especially without any honorific. The
proper way of addressing them is "master" or "teacher."
Another mistake is the repeated use of "Ara!" (an expression
used only in women's speech to show surprise) in an entirely
wrong way and place.

4-084.   ----------------. Of Nightingales that Weep. Illustrated by
          Haru Wells. New York: Crowell, 1974. 170 p. (6 up)

This is an exciting and sensitive story, set in the twelfth
century, about the young daughter of a warrior who grows to
womanhood after the death of her father. To provide for the
family, the mother marries a man who is not from the warrior
class. The girl's great gift for music eventually brings her
back into the upper levels of society as a lady-in-waiting
at court. She becomes the favorite of the Imperial family,
and accompanies them when they flee the capital at the
outset of the war. She is torn among her loyalties toward
the Imperial family, her clan, the Taira, her family, and
her lover, Hideo, the enemy spy. While she is away, her
mother and half-brother die of plague. After the war, she
comes back to the ruins of her stepfather's house, and she
marries him when she realizes the good human qualities in
him.

4-085.   ----------------. The Sign of the Chrysanthemum. New York:
          Crowell, 1974. 132 p. (5 up)

This story takes place in twelfth-century Japan. A boy named
Muna (which means "no name") goes to Kyoto, the capital of
Japan at that time, to look for his father. The only clue to
identify his father is a tattoo of a chrysanthemum. The boy
is given protection by a famous swordsmith. Sometimes the
story gets rather vague because of the way the conversations
are presented. A good, very Japanese, story.

4-086.   Peck, Helen E. and Dearmin, Jennie T. The Smiling Dragon.
          Illustrated by Lon Sevillia. Minneapolis; Denison, c.
          1963. Unpaged. (K-3)

Both the text and the illustrations are very inaccurate. The
text states many misconceptions and incorrect information as
facts. For example, it is not a fish kite as stated in the
book that swims in the sky on Boys' Day. It is a carp, made
of cloth, that is tied on a tall pole. In referring to
samurai spirit the text reads, "He was as determined as the
cherry blossoms that cling to the branches..." The cherry
blossom is a symbol of samurai spirit because it blossoms
for a short time and never clings to the branches. The
cherry blossoms symbolize the samurai's readiness to
sacrifice himself for lord or country without hesitation. Do
not use.

4-087.   Perkins, Lucy F. Japanese Twins. New York: Weatherhill,
          Walker, c. 1912, reprinted in 1968. 177 p. (3-5)

The daily lives of Japanese twins at the end of the 19th
century. The book attempts to explain Japanese culture. Much
of the illustrative and textual information, however, such
as the illustration showing children wearing zori in the
house or the one showing a bathtub with a chimney inside the
house, is inaccurate. Not recommended.

4-088.   Piggott, Juliet. Great Day in Japan: The Bigger Fish.
          Illustrated by Peter Thompson. New York: Abelard-Schuman,
          c. 1962. Unpaged. (K-3)

A story about the typical activities of two young Japanese
brothers on Boys' Festival Day, celebrated each year on May
5. Some activities cited, such as kite flying, are not
special to the Boys' Festival and some such as playing
battledore, are done only by girls on New Year's Day. Some
of the illustrations, such as the kimono, battledore
rackets, and kite designs, are not authentic.

4-089.   Roy, Ron. A Thousand Pails of Water. Pictures by Vo-Dinh
          Mai. New York: Knopf, c. 1978. Unpaged. (K-3)

Yukio, the son of a whale fisherman, finds a whale which is
trapped between two huge rocks and is about to die because
the tide is getting low. Fearing that the adults will kill
the whale if he tells them, the little boy promises to carry
1,000 pails of water to save the life of the trapped whale.
He becomes exhausted trying to fulfill his promise and when
the villagers find out why, they help the whale escape when
the tide comes in. Heartwarming story.

4-090.   Sakade, Florence, ed. The Japanese Twins Lucky Day: Picture
          Plays for Kindergarten, School, Home. Illustrated by Hanji
          Koyano. Rutland, VT.: Tuttle, c. 1964. 12 panels. (K-1)

Edited by Sakade into a picture play from an episode of Lucy
Perkins' The Japanese Twins, but actually it is almost a new
story. Through the seven-year-old Japanese twins' daily
lives, children will be able to learn what the everyday life
of Japanese children is like. The grandmother tells the
twins that it is going to be a lucky day for them when they
are leaving for school in the morning. After a long,
dragging day, they find out it really is a lucky day after
all because their mother comes home with a newborn baby boy.

4-091.   Say, Allen. The Bicycle Man. Oakland, CA: Parnassus Press,
         1982. Unpaged. (K-3)

Toward the end of a Sport's Day, an important event in
Japanese schools, two American soldiers come to a small
school in the mountains. The amazing tricks one of these
soldiers does on the principal's bicycle is a great finale
for the festivities. The story and the delicate and detailed
pen drawing illustrations complement each other very well.

4-092.   ----------------. The Feast of Lanterns. New York: Harper &
         Row, c. 1976. 57 p. (K-4)

A story of the adventures of two young brothers who live in
a fishing village on a small Japanese island. They take
their uncle's fishing boat and go to the mainland, which
they call "the better place," on the Feast of Lanterns, the
traditional festival of the dead. However, both of them find
that the reality is nothing like what they have dreamed of
for so long. This carefully thought out but very naturally
told story with authentic and detailed illustrations is
highly recommended.

4-093.   ----------------. The Ink-Keeper's Apprentice. New York:
         Harper & Row, c. 1979. 185 p. (5 up)

The story is about a young boy growing up in Japan right
after the War. Although this book is categorized in the
reference book under Japan, it does not particularly treat
things Japanese.

4-094.   Schuefftan, Kim. The Tengu's Thunder-Staff. Illustrations by
         Yasuo Segawa. Tokyo: Kodansha International, 1966.
         Unpaged. (1-5)

A young boy who lives alone with his grandmother deep in the
mountains of Japan has heard about tengu, the long-nosed,
dreadful-looking, and mischievous legendary creatures. One
day while at play, he is found by a tengu,
Ringoropyonpyontobijetplanekenchan, who has just awakened
from a sleep of over 100 years. Ringoro tengu is very
mischievous and tries all the tricks he can on this little

boy. But to his disappointment and surprise, the boy is not
only fearless, but even enjoys having tricks played on him!
Not only that, he runs away with Ringoro tengu's thunder
staff and plays tricks on Ringoro tengu. The boy causes
severe earthquakes and thunder with the staff. His hut, with
his grandmother in it, falls into a crevice caused by the
earthquakes. He realizes he has gone too far and returns the
staff to Ringoro tengu. The boy's grandmother, who is a good
sweetcake maker, invites Ringoro tengu for a taste of her
specialty. After that, they all become good friends. The
usage of "um" in the text is not a regular usage of this
interjection, but except for this small detail, this is an
enjoyable book for all children.

4-095.   Slobodkin, Louis. Yasu and the Strangers. New York:
          Macmillan, 1965. 34 p. (K-3)

Yasu, a little Japanese boy, goes on a school excursion with
his brother and his classmates. He becomes separated from
his group and meets an American who is also lost. Little
Yasu helps the American and they have many experiences.
Could also be used in social studies.

4-096.   Statler, Oliver. Japanese Inn. New York: Random House, c.
          1961, paperback edition published from University of
          Hawaii Press, 1982. xii, 365 p. (10 up)

The author traces the history of an old Japanese inn located
along a major transportation route which has been the scene
of some of Japan's most stirring historical events. The inn
is located along the Tokaido, the road which for centuries
has been the major highway between Tokyo and Kyoto, the
ancient capital of Japan. The history of Japan and the
history of the family which has owned the inn since its
founding are intertwined in a series of stories and
anecdotes. Illustrated with many well-selected old prints
and drawings which are a major interest of this author.

4-097.   Takahashi, Hiroyuki. The Foxes of Chironupp Island. Stories
          and pictures by Hiroyuki Takahashi. English translation by
          Ann King Herring. New York: Windmill Books and Dutton,
          1976. Unpaged. (K-2)

A touching story of parents' love among humans and animals,
and the sad effect of war on men. The text is written like
lyrics and the dream-like illustrations are certain to make
young children think.

4-098.   Takeichi, Yasoo. The Mightly Prince. Drawn by Yoshimasa
          Sejima. New York: Crown, c. 1971. Unpaged. (1-4)

This story is about a fierce prince. All he can do is fight.
After he has fought in all the wars, there is nothing for
him to do. He is angry, hated by everyone, and empty-
hearted. He comes to understand how joy and love are alike
by planting and caring for the seeds given to him by a
little girl. Well-told story with effective and powerful
illustrations. Only the last page is in full color, and has
a dramatic effect. The moral of the story is more universal
than Japanese, but the text is beautifully poetic. A very
good book.

4-099.   Takeyama, Michio. Harp of Burma. Library of Japanese
          Literature, translated from the Japanese by Howard
          Hibbett. Rutland, VT: Tuttle, c. 1966, 1982 printing. 132
          p. (7 up)

Translation of a beautiful and touching novel about a
company of young Japanese soldiers in Burma during World War
II. They are a close-knit group and they survived the war
because of their friendship and dedication to the group.
Immediately after their surrender to English troops at the
end of the war, one of the soldiers, Mizushima, agrees to
help the British, temporarily, in the hope of preventing the
death of more Japanese soldiers. As Mizushima travels across
Burma trying to rejoin his unit, he finds countless unburied
Japanese dead. Faced with a conflict between his strong
desire to rejoin his comrades and his growing need to do
something for his dead countrymen, he finally chooses to
remain in Burma as a Buddhist monk and bury the dead.
Strongly recommended.

4-100.   Tsuboi, Sakae. Twenty-Four Eyes. Tuttle Books. Translated by
          Akira Miura. Rutland, VT: Tuttle, c. 1983, 244 p. (3-12)

This is a touching story of an elementary school teacher and
her twelve pupils during the years 1926 to 1946. By
following the lives of innocent children through these
crucial years in recent Japanese history, the author points
out the inhumanity of war. This is a very convincing anti-
war novel. Although there are no illustrations, the book
would be enjoyed by people of all ages because the
translation is well done. The story was made into a movie in
Japan and was enjoyed by people of all ages. Highly
recommended.

4-101.   Uchida, Yoshiko. The Forever Christmas Tree. Illustrated by
          Kazue Mizumura. New York: Scribner, 1963. Unpaged. (K-3)

A Christmas story set in a small mountain village in Japan
where people have never celebrated Christmas or decorated a
Christmas tree. Takashi, a young boy, has nothing to do in
winter. Then one day, his older sister, Kaya, tells him what

she learned at school about Christmas. After listening to
the story, Takashi wants to have his own Christmas tree more
than anything else. On Christmas Eve, the brother and sister
make decorations for a Christmas tree, but there are not
enough to decorate a big tree. The only tree that is just
right belongs to Mr. Toda, nicknamed Old Mr. Thunder.
Finally, Takashi and Kaya decide to do a daring thing and
decorate the small fir tree planted by the entrance to Old
Mr. Thunder's house. Early Christmas morning, Mr. Toda finds
his little tree brightly decorated. he not only does not
become angry, but he invites the children to see it. Kaya
and Takashi bring all their friends. Everyone is happy to
see the Christmas tree for the first time, and Mr. Toda
gives the children permission to decorate his tree every
Christmas for as long as they like. Good illustrations of
Japanese houses and how children dress in winter. There are
some careless mistakes in otherwise good illustrations; the
dog named Shiro, which means "white", is shown as a black
dog; the text says the little girl's braids swing in the air
but the illustration shows her with short hair.

4-102.   ----------------. Hisako's Mysteries. Illustrated by Susan
          Bennett. New York: Scribner, c. 1969. 112 p. (4-9)

Hisako lives with her grandparents in Kyoto, Japan, since
both of her parents died when she was still a baby, or so
she was told. But her grandparents never talk about her
parents. On her twelfth birthday, Hisako receives some money
in the mail from an unidentified person. Before she can find
out who sent the money, she has a chance to travel to Tokyo
with her best friend's family. The night before she leaves,
her grandparents' housekeeper secretly hands Hisako an old
photograph of a young artist and tells her to look for him.
Another mystery! Soon after her exciting trip to Tokyo,
Hisako is involved in an accident. This near tragedy becomes
the starting point of the solution to all the mysteries
around Hisako. This is not particularly Japanese, but the
everyday life of the Japanese is depicted well.

4-103.   ----------------. In-Between Miya. Illustrated by Suzan
          Bennett. New York: Scribner, 1967. 128 p. (3-6)

Twelve-year-old Miya lives in a small village. She is the
third child in the family and has a younger brother. She
does not like being in-between in the family because she
sees only disadvantages to that position. She does not like
to live in the country, either. During summer vacation, her
sick aunt in Tokyo wants her to come to help with the
housework. She tries her best, but the responsibility is too
heavy for her, and she is sent back home. She feels as if
she is a complete failure, but with the wise guidance of her
parents and the help of her new friend from Tokyo, she gains

confidence and starts to understand and accept the simple
country life. Everyday family life in the countryside of
Japan is described in accurate detail. A good introduction
to Japan as well as a good story of a girl growing up.

4-104.   ----------------. Makoto, the Smallest Boy. New York:
Crowell, c. 1970. Unpaged. (1-4)

A story of Makoto, a third-grade Japanese boy. He is the
youngest in the family, the smallest in his class, the
slowest runner, and is never on a winning team. He has an
older brother, who is athletic and the leader of the winning
team. Makoto's inferiority complex cannot be soothed by
either parents. Eventually, Makoto receives consolation and
guidance from his old friend, Mr. Imai, who lives nearby and
is the best potter in Kyoto. Mr. Imai gives Makoto a
suggestion and a gift to help him find one thing he is very
good at. Makoto wins a blue ribbon for his oil painting at
school, and he gains confidence in himself. He learns that
if he works hard at one thing he likes, he can be the first.
With the help of good illustrations, the author describes
well the everyday life in an old Japanese town.

4-105.   ----------------. Rokubei and the Thousand Rice Bowls.
Illustrated by Kazue Mizumura. New York: Scribner, c.
1962. Unpaged. (K-4)

Rokubei, a farmer and a potter, likes to make pots and bowls
and cups. But the problem is that he cannot sell enough of
them, and as a result his house overflows with his pottery.
One day, his wife orders Rokubei to take all the pottery out
of the house. A great lord happens to pass by, and discovers
the pots. Recognition by this feudal lord changes the lives
of Rokubei's family members. They are transformed from poor
farmers to elegant, wealthy people, but the happiness they
enjoyed before is somewhat lost. To regain their former
happiness the family agrees to go back to the simple,
country life style. The story is not very smoothly told, but
it certainly presents an unmistakable Japanese value.
Humorous black-and-white illustrations match the mood of the
story.

4-106.   ----------------. Sumi and the Goat and the Tokyo Express.
Pictures by Kazue Mizumura. New York: Scribner, c. 1969.
42 p. (K-4)

Sumi's ninety-year-old friend, Mr. Oda, gets a goat. About
the same time a new railroad reaches Sugi, the village where
Sumi lives. But the trains only go through the village
without making a stop. One day, the goat gets out of the old
man's backyard and stops an express train heading toward
Tokyo. All the children are invited on board to see what the

inside of the train looks like. Lively illustrations
complement the warm humor of this story and show the
classroom in a Japanese village school clearly.

4-107.   ----------------. Sumi's Prize. Illustrated by Kazue
          Mizumura. New York: Scribner, c. 1964. Unpaged. (1-3)

A seven-year-old Japanese girl, Sumi, has never won a prize
and she wants to win one befofe she grows old. When her
teacher, who also happens to be the Mayor of the village,
announces the kite flying contest on New Year's Day, she
decides this is her chance. She works hard to make her own
kite, and she is doing well flying her kite on contest day
until the Mayor's silk top hat, which she adores, is swept
away by a gust of wind. She sacrifices her kite flying to
save the Mayor's top hat and for her action she receives a
prize from the Mayor. Village life in Japan is the setting
of this story. The illustrations match the story very well,
although Sumi's golden butterfly kite is red due to the
limitation of the use of color in the illustrations.

4-108.   ----------------. Sumi's Special Happening. Pictures by Kazue
          Mizumura. New York: Scribner, c. 1966. Unpaged. (1-4)

Seven-year-old Sumi cannot think of any birthday present for
her old friend, Mr. Oda. It is going to be his ninety-ninth
birthday so the present has to be something very special.
She asks around for suggestions, and the Mayor of the
village who also happens to be her teacher suggests giving
Mr. Oda some "happening." When a friend of her father comes
to her house for a visit and talks about his new job, Sumi
conceives a splendid idea of a special happening for Mr.
Oda's birthday. It turns out to be a delightful surprise
for, not only Mr. Oda, but for everyone in the village. The
illustrations by Kazue Mizumura capture the mood of Sumi and
everyone in the village and depicts the general surroundings
of the Japanese house and village life very well.

4-109.   ----------------. Takao and Grandfather's Sword. Illustrated
          by William M. Hutchinson. New York: Harcourt, c. 1958. 127
          p. (2-6)

Takao, a ten-year-old Japanese boy wants to help his father
at the potter's wheel and to fire the kiln. He is sometimes
impetuous and still cannot be trusted. He is too eager and
does not want to wait for his time, and that leads him into
real trouble, a disastrous fire in his father's workshop.
When he realizes what he has done to his father and family,
he sells his only valuable possession, the beautiful samurai
sword he inherited from his grandfather. He courageously
visits the people who might buy the sword from him, and
learns a great deal about sacrifice, loyalty, and

unhappiness, and grows into a responsible person. The story is well-told, and daily life in Japan is described well. Illustrations are mostly well done in black-and-white.

4-110.   Van Aken, Helen. Tatsu the Dragon. Illustrated by Yoshie Noguchi. Rutland, VT: Tuttle, 1966. 101 p. (1-4)

An adventurous fantasy of how Tatsu, a boy dragon made by two Japanese boys for a parade for a shrine festival, becomes a real dragon through courageous deeds. There are a few minor mistakes, but, in general, children will enjoy this fantasy. Good black-and-white illustrations.

4-111.   Whitney, Phyllis A. Secret of the Samurai Sword. Philadelphia: Westminster, c. 1958. 206 p. (5 up)

American children who are spending their summer vacation with their grandmother in a haunted house in Kyoto, Japan, solve the mystery of the samurai sword with their Japanese friends. The story is well told, with good descriptions of Japan, and is much more than a mystery. It is also a heartwarming story of friendship between children from different cultural and language backgrounds. Accurate and informative as well as enjoyable.

4-112.   Winthrop, Elizabeth. Journey to the Bright Kingdom. Illustrated by Charles Mikolaycak. New York: Holiday House, c. 1979. Unpaged. (4-6)

The mice of kakure-sato grant a blind woman temporary sight during the journey she and her daughter make to the mice's magical underground kingdom. This is an adaptation of a well-known Japanese folktale, The Rolling Rice Cakes. Good attractive illustrations and story.

4-113.   Wise, Winifred E. The Revolt of the Darumas. Illustrated by Beverly Komoda. New York: Parents' Magazine Press, c. 1970. 38 p. (2-4)

It is a Japanese custom to buy a daruma tumbler without eyes when someone has a wish to make. The person making the wish draws an eye on the daruma doll. The doll then works hard for the wish to come true to get itself another eye. When the wish comes true, the person draws the other eye on the doll. In this story, three children in the same family separately wish to go to a festival and each buys a daruma and paints one eye on the doll. The dolls are left in a room which has a tengu mask hanging on the wall. The tengu, an evil mythical creature with a long nose, laughs at the darumas because they only have one eye. The darumas remain silent but gain their revenge when the tengu, filled with rage after the children add the eyes on the darumas when

their wish comes true, fall off the wall and breaks his
nose. One of the children is incorrectly given the personal
name Kojima which is in actuality a last name.

4-114.   Yashima, Taro. Crow Boy. New York: Viking, c. 1955. 37 p.
          (K-3)

A sensitive story of a boy to whom no one paid any attention
except to ridicule him, and how one day he became a hero of
the school. This introverted little boy had a problem
adjusting to the school situation and was transformed into a
confident boy through a warm, understanding, teacher.
Through the teacher's help, the other children begin to
understand this boy's talents. The informative illustrations
in soft mixed colors are attractive. A very short, but
meaningful text will be enjoyed by children. This book could
also be used for the study of Japan in social studies.
Highly recommended.

4-115.   --------------. The Village Tree. Text and illustrations by
          T. Yashima. New York: Viking, c. 1953. 35 p. (K-2)

Well-constructed book with a simple and attractive style;
very informative about the lives of children in a small
village in Japan. Good and informative illustrations by the
author. While I do not think this is the use originally
intended, this book can be used for social studies as well
as for reading for fun.

4-116.   Yashima, Mitsu and Yashima, Taro. Plento to Watch. New York:
          Viking, c. 1954. 39 p. (K-3)

Very informative book about the everyday life of an old
Japanese village. The authors recorded the things and people
they used to watch on the way home from school. Full of good
and accurate observations revealing the warmth of the hearts
of the authors. Could be used for social studies.

4-117.   Yoshikawa, Eiji. Musashi. Translated from the Japanese by
          Charles S. Terry. Foreword by Edwin Reischauer. New York:
          Harper & Row/Kodansha International, c. 1981. xiii, 970 p.
          (10 up)

Eiji Yoshikawa was one of Japan's best-loved popular
writers. This work, which Reischauer calls the "Gone With
the Wind" of Japan, first appeared as a serial in a Japanese
newspaper in the 1930s. Musashi Miyamoto was an actual
historical person and is known as one of the best swordsmen
Japan has ever produced. This is the story of a young
reckless warrior, the only son of a good swordsman, who

becomes one of the most self-disciplined and renowned
swordsmen of his time. The combination of a love story and
samurai adventure makes this an exciting, appealing book.

4-118.   Zimelman, Nathan. A Good Morning's Work. Illustrated by
         Carol Rogers. Austin, TX: Steck-Vaughn, c. 1968. 32 p.
         (K-3)

The story is about Mitsuo Yamada's weeding of his family
garden one morning. He is told by his father to do the job,
and although the father keeps on reminding him, the boy is
too tender-hearted to pull out the weeds because he does not
want to disturb the spider's web, the bird's nest, the bees,
or frog's puddle. He ends up not doing much of what he is
supposed to have done, but he is very satisfied that he did
not disturb anything and calls his work "A good morning's
work." The story itself is funny and warm, but it is not
particularly Japanese. The boy in the illustrations wears a
Vietnamese hat, and nothing but his name is Japanese.

4-119.   ----------------. Look, Hiroshi! Woodcut illustration by Dan
         Quest. Nashville: Aurora Publisher, c. 1972. 28 p. (K-3)

A beautiful story of a young girl who likes fantasy and her
brother who is a typical, practical boy. Soon, the big
eight-year-old brother is influenced by his five-year-old
sister's imagination. It is a good story, but except for the
use of Japanese names, it is not necessarily Japanese.

Books Having Little or Nothing to do with Japan

Blackburn, Joyce. <u>Suki and the Invisible Peocock</u>. Grand Rapids, MI:
Zondervan, c. 1965.
Edogawa, Rampo. <u>Japanese Tales of Mystery and Imagination</u>. Rutland,
VT: Tuttle, 1956.
Garner, Alan. <u>A Cavalcade of Goblins</u>. New York: Walck, 1969.
Godden, Rumer. <u>Little Plum</u>. New York: Viking Press, 1963.
Hamada, Hirosuke. <u>Little Mouse who Tarried</u>. New York: Parent's
Magazine, 1971.
Ishiguro, Kazuo. <u>A Pale View of Hills</u>. New York: Putnum's Sons, c.
1982.
Itaya, Kikuo. <u>Tengu Child</u>. Carbondale, IL: Southern Illinois
University Press, 1983.
Iwasaki, Chihiro. <u>Staying Home Alone on a Rainy Day</u>. New York:
McGraw-Hill, 1969.
Kasuya, Masahiro. <u>The Smallest Christmas Tree</u>. New York: Ryer,
Milton, 1981.
Kherdian, David. <u>Beyond Two Rivers</u>. New York: Greenwillow, c. 1981.
Kijima, Hajime. <u>Little White Hen</u>. New York: Harper-Brace, 1967.
Kimishima, Hisako. <u>Lum Fu and the Golden Mountain</u>. New York: Parent's
Magazine, 1971.
Kirkup, James. <u>The Magic Drum</u>. New York: Knopf, c. 1973.
Kishida, Eriko. <u>The Lion and the Bird's Nest</u>. New York: Crowell,
1973.
Maeda, Mieko. <u>How Rabbitt Tricked His Friends</u>. New York: Parent's
Magazine, c. 1969.
Mizumura, Kazue. <u>If I Were a Mother</u>. New York: Crowell, 1967.
Morse, Samuel French. <u>Sea Sums</u>. Illustrated by Fuku Akino. Boston:
Little, Brown, 1970.
Myers, Steven. <u>The Enchanted Sticks</u>. Illustrated by Donna Daimond.
New York: Coward, McCann & Geoghegan, c. 1979.
Nakatani, Chiyoko. <u>My Day on the Farm</u>. New York: Crowell, 1976.
Nye, Robert. <u>Out of This World and Back Again</u>. Indianapolis: Bobbs-
Merrill, c. 1978.
Sasaki, Tazu. <u>Golden Thread</u>. Rutland, VT: Tuttle, c. 1968.
Taylor, Mark. <u>The Fisherman and the Goblet</u>. Illustrated by Taro
yashima.
Uchida, Risako. <u>Sparrow's Magic</u>. New York: Parent's Magazine, 1970.
Uchida, Yoshiko. <u>A Jar of Dreams</u>. New York: Atheneum, 1982.
----------. <u>Samurai of Gold Hill</u>. New York: Scribner, 1972.
Withers, Carl. <u>I Saw a Rocket Walk a Mile</u>. New York: Holt, Rinehart &
Winston, 1965.
Wolkstein, Diane. <u>Lazy Stories</u>. New York: Seabury Press, c. 1976.
Yashima, Mitsu and Taro. <u>Momo's Kitten</u>. New York: Viking Press, 1961.
Yashima, Taro. <u>Umbrella</u>. New York: Viking Press, 1958.

5. POETRY

5-001. Andrews, James David. Full Moon is Rising: "Lost Haiku" of Matsuo Basho (1644-1694) and Travel Haiku of Matsuo Basho: A New Rendering. Boston: Branden Press, c. 1976. 94 p. (10 up)

New translation of the famous haiku master's poetry. It looks as if the renditions are simply a reworking of another English translation.

5-002. Baron, Virginia Olsen, ed. The Seasons of Times: Tanka Poetry of Ancient Japan. Illustrated by Yasuhide Kobashi, New York: Dial Press, c. 1968. 63 p. (5 up)

Most of the poems in this book were selected from the ancient Kokinshu and Manyoshu and are poems by people from all walks of life. These may be a little difficult for grade-school children because of length (in Japanese the 5,7,5,7,7, syllable scheme is the poetic form of the tanka). The poems are more descriptive and complicated than haiku and would be good for children who are already familiar with the haiku form. Good introduction at the beginning of the volume. Arrangement done by the seasons of the year. An index of poets is included.

5-003. Behn, Harry, ed. and trans. Cricket Songs: Japanese Haiku with Pictures Selected from Sesshu and Other Japanese Masters. New York: Harcourt, 1964. 64 p. (4 up)

A well-selected and well-translated collection of Japanese haiku, the seventeen-syllable poems. Most poems are simple enough for children to understand. A useful combination of good Japanese painting and poems.

5-004.   ----------------. ed. and trans. <u>More Cricket Songs: Japanese
          Haiku</u>. Illustrated with pictures by Japanese masters. New
          York: Harcourt, 1971. 64 p. (5 up)

          Good new collection of <u>haiku</u> poems by the
          compiler/translator of <u>Cricket Songs</u>. Drawn from the work of
          about thirty poets. Simple, delicate, serene, illustrations
          contribute to the mood of this new collection. Good
          translation.

5-005.   Cassedy, Sylvia, ed. & trans. <u>Birds, Frogs, and Moonlight:
          Haiku</u>. Translated and compiled by Sylvia Cassedy and
          Suetake Kunihiro. Illustrated by Vo-Dinh. Calligraphy by
          Koson Okamura. New York: Doubleday, c. 1967. 47 p. (K-4)

          A bilingual collection of <u>haiku</u> about animals in nature
          especially for young children. For each poem, the Japanese
          writing and romanized original poems are given along with
          English translation. Unfortunately there are many mistakes
          in both text and illustrations in this otherwise lovely
          collection. There are three mistakes of romanization, and a
          few poems have a difference in text between the Japanese and
          romanized versions. Some poems do not match the
          illustrations. One poem talks about slippers, but the
          illustration depicts a geta, a Japanese wooden clog. An
          inaccurate and carelessly compiled book, but it may
          encourage young children's imagination and creativity for
          writing poems. Includes a note on <u>haiku</u>.

5-006.   DeForest, Charlotte B. <u>The Prancing Pony: Nursery Rhymes
          from Japan</u>. Adapted into English verse for children by
          C.G. DeForest. <u>Kusa-e</u> illustrations by Keiko Hida. New
          York: Walker, c. 1967. 63 p. (K-6)

          DeForest selected and translated these nursery rhymes and
          folk poetry collected by Tasaku Harada from all over Japan.
          Over fifty nursery rhymes are included in this charming
          collection. It is a difficult task to translate nursery
          rhymes and retain the meaning and flavor of the original,
          but the translator has done a superb job. Simple but very
          expressive paper-cut illustrations using Japanese rice paper
          are extremely effective. Children will enjoy both the poems
          and the pictures while exercising their imaginations.

5-007.   <u>Don't Tell the Scarecrow, and Other Japanese Poems by Issa,
          Yayu, Kikaku and Other Japanese Poets</u>. Illustrations by
          Talivaldis Stubis. New York: Scholastic, c. 1969. Unpaged.
          (K-4)

          The illustrator of this book simply borrowed translated
          poems from various collections of Japanese <u>haiku</u> and did not
          give proper credit to the translators. At least one poem is

attributed to the wrong poet. Careless work, and
illustrations lack authenticity. Poems could be read to the
class.

5-008. Fujiwara no Sadaie, ed. The Little Treasury of One Hundred
People, One Poem Each. Translated by Tom Galt. Princeton,
NJ: Princeton University Press, c. 1982. xii 106 p. (10
up)

A good translation of the most popular Japanese anthology of
waka (tanka) poems, Ogura Hyakunin Isshu, or one hundred
people, one poem each. The book is bilingual and each poem
is written in Japanese calligraphy followed by a
transliteration, a translation, and a short commentary. A
very short introduction to this collection, which is often
played as a card game in Japan. Appended with an index and a
glossary of poets.

5-009. Fukuda, Hanako. Wind in My Hand. With the editorial
assistance of Mark Taylor, Haiku translations by Hanako
Fukuda, illustrations by Lydia Cooley. San Carlos, CA:
Golden Gate Junior Books, 1970. 61 p. (4-6)

A moving well-told biography of Issa, a celebrated Japanese
haiku poet of the Edo period, based on his autobiography and
his poems. The name of Issa's teacher, Rokuzaemon, is
incorrectly spelled as Rokuazemon throughout the book.

5-010. A Hundred Verses from Old Japan: Being a Translation of the
Hyaku-nin-Isshiu. Translated by William N. Porter,
Rutland, VT: Tuttle, 1979. xiv, unpaged (10 up)

Originally published in England in 1909, this is one of the
oldest translations of the most famous Japanese anthology of
tanka (31-syllable poetry), Hyakunin Issu or "Single verses
by a hundred people." The poems were written between 670
A.D. and 1235, when the anthology was compiled. The
collection consists almost entirely of love poems and
descriptive poems. Each poem is presented first in
romanized Japanese, then followed by a black-and-white
illustration, the poet's name, the translation, and finally
a note about the poem, the poet, and sometimes the
illustration. Includes a good introduction. Excellent
translations:

5-011. Kobayashi, Issa. A Few Flies and I: Haiku by Issa. Selected
by Jean Merrill and Ronni Solbert from translations by
R.H. Blyth and Nobuyuki Yuasa. Illustrated by Ronni
Solbert. new York: Random House, c. 1969. 96 p. (4 up)

Good introductory words about Issa, the Japanese haiku poet
of the eighteenth century at the beginning of the volume.
The credit of good translation belongs to Blyth and Yuasa.
The illustrations are small and give the feeling of haiga
drawings that accompany haiku. Good selection of Issa's
poems which are easy enough for children. Children will feel
the warmness of this master's heart by listening to these
poems. Could be used in social studies for units such as
understanding others and our friends, animals, etc.

5-012.   Lewis, Richard, ed. In a Spring Garden. Pictures by Ezra
          Jack Keats. New York: Dial Press, c. 1965. Unpaged. (K-6)

Arranged in the order of one spring day, morning to evening.
A lovely collection of twenty-three Japanese haiku in a
picture book format, selected from the works of famous
Japanese haiku poets from the seventeenth century to the
modern period. Illustrations match the mood of the poems.
This could be enjoyed by very small children as well as
grownups. Translations are collected from many books of
haiku poetry.

5-013.   ----------------. The Moment of Wonder: A Collection of
          Chinese and Japanese Poetry. Illustrated with paintings by
          Chinese and Japanese masters. New York: Dial Press, c.
          1964. 138 p. (5 up)

A collection of Chinese and Japanese poems about nature and
the seasons from many centuries. The only trouble with this
book is that there is no way of knowing whether a poem is
Chinese or Japanese unless the reader knows the difference
between Chinese and Japanese names. There are many poems
which children will love.

5-014.   ----------------. Of This World: A Poet's Life in Poetry.
          Photographs by Helen Buttfield. New York: Dial Press, c.
          1968. 94 p. (5 up)

The life of Issa, a famous eighteenth-century haiku poet, is
treated in this book, along with many of his warm and
humanistic poems. Well-organized book. Excellent
photography.

5-015.   ----------------. There Are Two Lives: Poems by Children of
          Japan. Translated by Haruno Kimura. New York: Simon and
          Schuster, 1970. 96 p. (1-6)

Approximately seventy poems selected from among published
Japanese children's poems are arranged by topic such as
family, play, school, creatures, nature, and thoughts. Full

of imaginative, keen, observant, and refreshing poems.
Children are sure to enjoy them. Illustrated with pictures
drawn by Japanese children.

5-016.   ----------------. The Way of Silence: The Prose and Poetry of
Basho. Photographs by Helen Buttfield. New York: Dial
Press, c. 1970. 111 p. (5-9)

This is a companion volume to Of This World: A Poet's Life
in Poetry (Kobayashi Issa, 1968). The life of Basho,
originator of the haiku style and the most famous haiku poet
of the seventeenth century, is treated in this book along
with his poems and prose. Well-selected poems and prose,
well translated, and black-and-white photographs are nicely
mingled to present an interpretation and insight into the
life of a great Japanese poet and illustrate his oneness
with nature.

5-017.   Matsuo, Basho. A Haiku Journey: Basho's "Narrow Road to the
Far North". Translated by Dorothy Britton. Photographs by
Dennis Stock. New York: Kodansha International, 1980. 124
p. (10 up)

Originally published in 1974. The photographer spent a year
in Japan recreating in pictures Basho's journey to The
Narrow Path to the Far North. His tremendous success is
obvious in the exquisite photographs in this book. The color
photographs match perfectly with the poetics of Basho's text
and poems. The translations of both text and poem are
excellent. Highly recommended.

5-018.   Modern Japanese Poetry. Asian and Pacific Writing: 9
Translated by James Kirkup and edited by A.R. Davis.
Australia: University of Queensland Press, 1978. lxii, 323
p. (12 up)

Excellent translation of modern Japanese poetry done by
Kirkup, himself an established poet who has lived in Japan
for years.

5-019.   One Hundred Famous Haiku. Selected and translated into
English by Daniel C. Buchanan. Elmsford, NY: Japan
Publications, c. 1973. 120 p. (9 up)

Each haiku is written in romanized and traditional Japanese
writing along with its translation. An interpretation and
explanatory notes are also given. Generally good, but
several of the poems are misinterpreted. For example. page
15 "Nio no Umi" is interpreted as Two-Deva-King-Lake. Nio is
a name of dub-chick or greve. Page 21, hoshi-zuki-yo is
interpreted as stars in the moonlight. But this phrase means

the night the skies are bright with the lights of stars but
with no moon. Also the interpretation of the <u>haiku</u> on pages
22, 53, 57, 60, and 90 are incorrect.

5-020.   Rexroth, Kenneth and Atsumi, Ikuko, ed. and trans. <u>The
          Burning Heart: Women Poets of Japan</u>. Continuum Book. new
          York: Seabury Press, 1977. vii 184 p. (10 up)

All types of poems by seventy-seven women poets from all
periods of Japanese hitory are collected in this anthology.
Notes on each poet and a brief survey of the women poets of
Japan are included. Appended with a table of Japanese
historical periods.

5-021.   Ryokan. <u>One Robe, One Bowl: The Zen Poetry of Ryokan</u>.
          Translated and introduced by John Stevens. New York:
          Weatherhill, c. 1977. 85 p. (10 up)

The book includes 100 chinese-style and 103 Japanese-style
poems by the famous, excentric Zen priest, Ryokan. The
introduction discusses this priest/poet's life and
character, the Zen he practiced, and his poems. The
translator tried to retain the original fresh and direct
flavor of Ryokan's poems by avoiding refined poetic
expressions and by translating them into colloquial English.
A bibliography, and an index of titles and first lines are
included.

5-022.   Sato, Hiroaki and Watson, Burton, ed. and trans. <u>From the
          Country of Eight Islands: An Anthology of Japanese Poetry</u>.
          With an introduction by Thomas Rimer. Seattle: University
          of Washington Press, c. 1981. xliv, 652 p. (10 up)

Well-selected samples of all forms of Japanese poetry from
all periods of Japanese history are collected in this
ambitious anthology. The poems are divided into five
sections by period. There is a good introduction by Thomas
Rimer, a specialist in Japanese literature. It is a
convenient and useful volume.

5-023.   Shiffert, Edith Marcombe and Sawa, Yuki, comp. and trans.
          <u>Anthology of Modern Japanese Poetry</u>. Rutland, VT: Tuttle,
          c. 1972. 195 p. (5 up)

This is a collection of modern free-style poems, <u>tanka</u>
(thirty-one syllable poetry) and <u>haiku</u>. There is a good
lengthy introduction to the history of Japanese poetry and
the development of modern poetry. Poems by forty-nine modern
poets are divided into three sections: free verse, <u>tanka</u>,
and <u>haiku</u>. This collection is intended as an extension of
what has already been translated and introduced to Western
readers and the translators felt free to choose what they

particularly found significant and amenable to translation. All in all, this is a good representation of modern Japanese poetry. The poet's name is given both in romanized form and in Japanese. At the end of the volume, there is a biographical note on each poet in the order of appearance in the text. There is also a well-selected bibliography of English language publications and an index.

5-024.   Stewart, Harold. A Chime of Windbells: A Year of Japanese
          Haiku in English Verse. Rutland, VT: Tuttle, c. 1969, 1981
          printing. 236 p. (7 up)

This anthology of haiku is divided into the four seasons with a short section on the New Year. For the difficult haiku, explanatory notes have been added at the back of the book; there is also an extensive essay on haiku by the translator. Attractively illustrated with colored haiga, paintings done especially to accompany haiku. Includes a bibliography and an index of authors and titles.

5-025.   ----------------. A Net of Fireflies: Japanese Haiku and
          Haiku Paintings. With verse translations and an essay by
          Harold Stewart. Rutland, VT: Tuttle, c. 1960, 1981
          printing. 180 p. (7 up)

Three hundred and twenty haiku by many poets are included in this collection, as are thirty-three excellent full-page color haiga, or haiku paintings. The haiku are divided into four seasons and arranged from spring to winter. Each haiku is given a title. The haiga, except for one which was especially drawn for this book, were selected and reproduced from the Gendai Haigashu (Collection of Modern Haiku Paintings), which was published in Tokyo from 1915-1917. There is an extensive essay on haiku and haiga by the translator/compiler. Also notes, a bibliography, and an index of poets and titles are included. A very attractive book.

5-026.   The Ten Thousand Leaves: A Translation of the Man'yoshu,
          Japan's Premier Anthology of Classical Poetry. Princeton
          Library of Asian Translations. Translated by Ian Hideo
          Levy. Princeton, NJ: Princeton University Press, 1981-. v.
          1-. (9 up)

This is a complete and excellent translation of the Man'yoshu, Japan's first anthology of poetry. The poems, written by people from all walks of life, were compiled in the eighth century. There is an excellent and extensive introduction by the translator.

5-027.   Watson, Burton, trans. Ryokan: Zen Monk-Poet of Japan.
          Translations from the Oriental Classics. New York:
          Columbia University Press, 1977. 126 p. (7 up)

Ryokan, a Zen monk, master calligrapher, and poet who lived
from 1757 to 1831, is a household name in Japan, and his
poetry is widely read by children and adults alike. He
expressed his personal feelings in much of his poetry which
is easy to understand. Forty-three of his Chinese-style
poems and eighty-three of his Japanese-style poems are
included. There is also an excellent biography of Ryokan
included.

5-028.   Wright, Harold, ed. and trans. Ten Thousand Leaves: Love
          Poems From the Manyoshu. New York: Shambhala, 1979. 94 p.
          (10 up)

These poems were selected from the Manyoshu, the oldest
collection of Japanese poems. Not illustrated.

5-029.   Yosa, Buson. Haiku Master Buson. Translations from the
          Writings of Yosa Buson--Poet and Artist--With Related
          Materials. By Yuki Sawa and Edith Marcombe Shiffert. San
          Francisco: Heian International, c. 1978. 178 p. (7 up)

Buson is one of the three most famous haiku poets along with
Basho and Issa, but this is the first book in English
devoted entirely to his work. Of his 3,000 haiku, 375 are
translated here. The haiku are grouped by season and
presented in both the Japanese original and English
translation. The introduction explains the seasons of haiku
and includes an essay on Buson and his writings, a brief
biography, and a record of his last days by one of his
disciples. Some of Buson's other writings and letters are
also included. There is both an English and Japanese
bibliography. The English bibliography is not devoted
exclusively to Buson. The Japanese bibliography is
excellent.

          Books Having Little or Nothing to do with Japan

Atwood, Ann. Haiku: The Mood of Earth. New York: Scribner, c. 1971.
          Unpaged.
----------. Haiku-Vision in Poetry and Photography. New York:
          Scribner, c. 1977. Unpaged.
----------. My Own Rhythm: An Approach to Haiku. New York: Scribner,
          1973. Unpaged.
Caudill, Rebecca. Come Along! Illustrated by Ellen Raskin. New York:
          Holt, Rinehart 7 Winston, 1969.
Inoue, Yukitoshi. Leaves in the Sun. New York: Weatherhill, c. 1967.
          95 p.
Klinge, Gunther. Day into Night. Selected and adapted by Ann Atwood.
          Rutland, VT: Tuttle, 1980. 180 p.
----------. Drifting with the Moon. Selected and adapted by Ann
          Atwood into English. Rutland, VT: Tuttle, 1978. 120 p.

Matsumoto, Toshiaki, comp. Our Big Teacher and Other Japanese
     Children's Poems. Translated by Yuzuru Katagiri. Tokyo:
     Shonen Shashin Shinbunsha, c. 1963. 32 p.
Mizumura, Kazue. Flower, Moon, Snow: A Book of Haiku. New York:
     Crowell, c. 1977. 48 p.
Roche, A.K. The City in Haiku. New York: Prentice Hall, c. 1970. 32
     p.

6. FOLKLORE AND LEGEND

6-001. Bartoli, Jennifer. The Story of the Grateful Crane: A Japanese Folktale. Illustrated under the direction of Kozo Shimizu. Chicago: Whitman, 1977. Unpaged. (K-2)

This is one of the most popular folktales in Japan. One day an old man saves a trapped crane. That night a beautiful young girl comes to the hut of the poor old man and his wife and asks to become their adopted daughter because she has no parents. The couple was delighted. Some time later, the girl offers to weave cloth which the couple can sell but only on condition that no one sees her weave. The old woman eventually breaks the promise and finds out that the girl is actually the crane. Because her true identity is revealed, the girl changes back into a crane and leaves the couple. The illustrations are full-color photographs of low-relief sculpture made of wood, fabric, and paper, which give the illustrations a special quality.

6-002. Brenner, Barbara. Little One Inch. Illustrated by Fred Brenner. New York: Coward, McCann & Geoghegan, c. 1977. 32 p. (K-3)

The story is based on Little One Inch (see Ishii, Issun Boshi), but with the addition of other legendary Japanese characters, the kappa and tengu. The author has changed this tale drastically and claims "to take from the past and shape the old legend in a new way." Hair styles in the illustrations are that of the Edo period's high-rank prostitute's. One mistake is that the boat depicted in the illustrations is a rice bowl made of earthenware, which will not float in the water, instead of a soup bowl made of curved wood.

6-003.   Bryant, Sara Cone. The Burning Rice Fields. With pictures by
         Mamoru Funai. New York: Holt, Rinehart and Winston, c.
         1963. 24 p. (K-2)

         The wisdom of an old man saves the lives of all the people
         in a small Japanese village from a tidal wave. Good, clear,
         authentic drawings with a good, simple, short story. This
         book is based on Lafcadio Hearn's Gleanings in Buddha-
         Fields.

6-004.   Carpenter, Francis. People from the Sky: Ainu Tales from
         Northern Japan. Illustrated by Betty Fraser. New York:
         Doubleday, c. 1972. 107 p. (4-6)

         Legends and stories told among the Ainu who were the
         aborigines of Japan and now are a minority group living in
         Hokkaido, the northern island. Both text and illustrations
         are very good and accurate. The book is based on research on
         the stories collected in the nineteenth century; sources are
         included in the bibliography. We should have more of this
         type of translation.

6-005.   Dobrin, Arnold. Taro and the Sea Turtles: A Tale of Japan.
         New York: Coward-McCann, c. 1966. Unpaged. (K-3)

         It is difficult to be sure that this really is a tale of
         Japan as the author claims. It is at the most an adaptation
         of the story about Urashima Taro, the fisherman who saved a
         turtle's life and as a reward was invited to the turtle's
         underwater palace. In this version, Taro, the son of a poor
         Buddhist priest, saves a turtle's life by buying it from a
         fisherman and returning it to the ocean. Later, when Taro's
         boat is at sea in the middle of the storm and when he is
         being robbed by the pirates, the grateful turtle helps him.
         The story is not particularly bad, but the illustrations are
         very bad. They are full of stereotypical mistakes such as
         Western bathrobes being shown as kimonos, and pirates
         wearing Chinese clothing and pigtails.

6-006.   Dolch, Edward W. and Dolch, Marguerite P. Stories from
         Japan. Folklore of the World Books. Champaign, IL: Garrard
         Press, c. 1960. vii, 168 p. (2-8)

         This collection has twenty entries of folktales and myths
         from Japan. The whole book is like loosely capped verses;
         often one story is divided into scenes and the scenes are
         entered as if they are separate stories without any
         indication that they are only part of a tale. The stories
         are written accurately and clearly in easy to read English.
         Good color illustrations.

6-007.   Dorson, Richard M. Folk Legends of Japan. Rutland, VT:
          Tuttle, 1962. 256 p. (9 up)

          This book was originally intended for the study of Japanese
          folklore. One hundred and twenty-two folktales are
          classified by subject, such as priests, temples and shrines,
          monsters, spirits, transformations etc. Many famous tales
          such as "Earless Ho-ichi," are included. Each tale is
          prefaced with detailed explanations and references. Detailed
          bibliography.

6-008.   Durham, Mae. Tobei: A Japanese Folktale. Illustrated by
          Mitsu Yashima. New York: Bradbury, c. 1974. Unpaged. (1-3)

          A tall tale from Japan retold. Tobei is good at digging imo,
          a long, edible root like a yam. One day, he finds an imo and
          digs day after day with the help of his friends and
          neighbors. When finally they pull out the long imo, Tobei
          falls into the deep hole. A wise man of the village suggests
          making a poultice to pull Tobei out of the hole just as the
          poultice draws pain from the body. The poultice works, but
          it is too strong and Tobei is blown to the roof of a temple.
          Priests try to catch Tobei on a quilt when he jumps down,
          but the jump is so powerful that the priests holding the
          quilt knock their heads and the sparks from that collision
          cause a fire. It is a funny, tall tale children will enjoy.
          The illustrations are blurred and it is difficult to see
          anything specifically Japanese in them.

6-009.   Edmonds, I.G. The Case of the Marble Monster and Other
          Stories. New York: Scholastic Book Services, 1969.

          See Ooka the Wise: Tales of Old Japan.

6-010.   ----------------. Ooka the Wise: Tales of Old Japan.
          Illustrated by Sanae Yamazaki. Indianapolis: Bobbs-
          Merrill, 1961. 96 p. (3-8)

          This is a collection of seventeen tales about the legendary
          Judge Ooka of the Edo period. The wily Ooka always manages
          to find out the truth and to solve seemingly insoluble
          problems. Most of the stories are authentic, but the author
          has a tendency to make small unnecessary changes which lead
          to mistakes. This book was more recently published by
          Scholastic Book Service under the title The Case of the
          Marble Monster and Other Stories in 1969.

6-011.   ----------------. The Possible Impossible of Ikkyu the Wise.
          Illustrated by Robert Byrd. Philadelphia: Macrae Smith, c.
          1971. 121 p. (4 up)

The tale of Ikkyu, a priest who has the wisdom of Solomon. The story is all right, but there are some mistakes in the text. The author invented all the names except Ikkyu, and although they are all Japanese, none are for priests or abbots, nor for students for the priesthood. The author repeatedly uses <u>kozu</u> to mean "student for the priesthood" instead of the correct word, <u>kozo</u>, which means literally "little priest." The head priest is always called "Oshosan," and never Mr. So-and-so; in addition, there are redundant expressions such as Kamogawa River, which means "Kamo-river River."

6-012. Fisher, Sally. <u>The Tale of the Shining Princess</u>. A Studia Book. New York: Metropolitan Museum of Art and the Viking Press, 1980. 70 p. (2-9)

Adapted from a translation of a tenth-century story by Donald Keene. A childless old man finds a tiny, shining baby girl in a bamboo grove and takes her home to raise. When she reaches adulthood, she has five suitors. She assigns each suitor an impossible task and promises to marry the suitor who succeeds. The exquisite illustrations are reproduced from an eighteenth-century edition of <u>Taketori monogatari</u> (Tale of the Bamboo Cutter) held by the Metropolitan Museum of Art. One of the best books.

6-013. <u>Folk Tales from Asia: For Children Everywhere</u>. New York: Weatherhill, c. 1975- v. 1-. (K-4)

Only a small portion of this collection is made up of Japanese folktales, but those included are good tales and well-translated with good illustrations.

6-014. Francis, Frank. <u>Timimoto's Great Adventure</u>. Holiday House Book. Written and Illustrated by Frank Francis. New York: Holiday House, c. 1969. Unpaged. (K-2)

This claims to be a "traditional Japanese tale of 4-inch tall Timinoto and his great victory over the dreaded ogre," but it appears to be a mixture of the stories of <u>Issun Boshi</u>, the Inchling, and Thumbelina. The illustrations are mostly in the Chinese style. Except for a mountain which looks like Mt. Fuji and the cherry blossoms, nothing in the story is really Japanese, including the name of the hero. Hopelessly stereotyped.

6-015. Goodman, Robert B. <u>Issunboshi</u>. Illustrated by George Suyeoka. Adapted from the original folktales by Robert E. Goodman and R. Spicer. Edited by Ruth Tabrah. Honolulu: Island Heritage, c. 1974. Unpaged. (K-2)

A popular tale which is the Japanese version of Tom Thumb.
(see Ishii, Issun Boshi) Both the retelling of the tale and
the illustrations are good. At the end of the book, the
score of the song of Issunboshi and an illustrated
explanation of Japanese items which appeared in the book are
provided.

6-016.   ----------------. Kaguya Hime: The Shimmering Princess.
Illustrated by George Suyeoka; adapted by Robert Goodman
and Robert A. Spicer, edited by Victor Johnson. Norfolk
Island, Australia: Island Heritage, c. 1974. 37 p. (2-4)

The story of the shining princess (see Fisher, The Tale of
the Shining Princess above). The illustrations in this
version sometimes mistakenly depict the nobleman suitors as
warriors. In general, however, a well-told story matched
with good illustrations.

6-017.   ---------------- and Spicer, Robert A. Urashima Taro. Edited
by Ruth Tabrah and illustrated by George Suyeoka.
Honolulu: Island Heritage, c. 1973. Unpaged. (1-6)

Good authentic illustrations and fairly good text. This is
another version of the well-known Japanese folktale,
Urashima the Fisherman. Appended with a score of the song of
Urashima Taro.

6-018.   Harris, Rosemary. The Child in the Bamboo Grove. Illustrated
by Errol Le Cain. New York: Phillips, c. 1971. Unpaged.
(4-6)

The story of the shining princess (see Fisher, The Tale of
the Shining Princess above). The reteller made many
unnecessary changes, adding details which are historically
incorrect. For example, one suitor's hobby was supposed to
be writing haiku, a poetic form which did not come into
existence until several centuries after the time of the
tale. Most of the illustrations are acceptable, but they are
a mixture of styles from woodblock prints and paintings of
different periods.

6-019.   Haviland, Virginia. Favorite Fairy Tales Told in Japan.
Illustrated by George Suyeoka. Boston: Little, Brown, c.
1967. 89 p. (2-5)

Five well-known fairy tales from Japan are included in this
small collection. Reasonably accurate and well-told, but
there is some shaky translation, such as "Honorable father,
honorable mother," and incorrect use of Japanese words such
as yo, banzai. This book is one of the earliest works to
record the sources of the stories. Should be used with
caution.

6-020.   Hearn, Lafcadio. The Boy Who Drew Cats: And Other Tales.
          Introduced by Pearl S. Buck. Illustrated by Manabu C.
          Saito. New York: Macmillan, 1963. v, 42 p. (2-6)

          Seven folktales from Japan are retold by Lafcadio Hearn in
          this oversized volume. There is an excellent introduction
          about the book and Hearn by Pearl Buck. The text is well-
          written and is accompanied by many authentic, full-color
          illustrations done by a Japanese artist.

6-021.   ---------------. Earless Ho-ichi: A Classic Japanese Tale of
          Mystery. With an introduction by Donald Keene.
          Illustrations by Masakazu Kuwata. Tokyo: Kodansha
          International, c. 1966. Unpaged. (5 up)

          A blind biwa (Japanese lute) player, Hoichi, lives with a
          priest in a Buddhist temple. He is known chiefly by his
          skillful recitation, to the accompanyment of the biwa, of
          the Tale of Heike, the story of the war between two warrior
          clans for control of the country in the twelfth century. The
          very temple he is staying in was built to appease the dead
          who perished during the final battle of the war at Dan-no-
          Ura. One night, when the priest was gone, someone comes to
          take Hoichi to perform for some nobles. He plays so well
          that the nobles want him to come back and play again, and
          they forbid Hoichi to say anything about this. The people of
          the temple find out about Hoichi's nocturnal concerts and
          realize that this audience consists of the dead Heike
          nobility. To prevent Hoichi from being taken to the world of
          the dead, the priest and his acolyte write the holy texts of
          Buddhism all over Hoichi's body except for his ears...
          Kuwata's exquisite and powerful illustrations combining the
          techniques of paper-cutting and woodcut-prints is the
          perfect complement to this simple but powerful story.
          Keene's introduction provides the background to truly
          appreciate this story. Most highly recommended.

6-022.   ---------------. In Ghostly Japan. Tuttle Books. Rutland,
          VT: Tuttle, 1979. 256 p. (9 up)

          Twelve ghost stories are beautifully and skillfully retold
          by Hearn in this collection of Japanese ghost stories.
          Japanese ghost stories are very different from those of the
          Western world and would be interesting to the Western
          reader. Some illustrations.

6-023.   ---------------. Kwaidan: Stories and Studies of Strange
          Things. With an introduction by Oscar Lewis. Illustrated
          by Yasumasa Fujita. New York: Dover Publications, 1968.
          xii, 113 p. (7 up)

Seventeen kwaidan, weird and scary tales, were collected and
told by Hearn, who showed a special taste for this type of
stories even before he went to Japan. All of them are very
Japanese and very well-told. Essays on insects by Hearn are
also included. There is an interesting and detailed
introduction about Lafcadio Hearn by Lewis.

6-024.   Herring, Ann. The Grateful Crane. Picture Story Series.
          Direction by Kozo Shimizu. Tokyo: Gakken, c. 1972.
          Unpaged. (k-2)

          A version of The Grateful Crane. (see Bartoli). Beautiful
          English text. Authentic, artistic, and expressive
          photographs add to the story. Highly recommended.

6-025.   Hodges, Margaret. The Wave. Adapted from Lafcadio Hearn's
          Gleanings in Buddha-Fields. Illustrated by Blair Lent.
          Boston: Houghton, Mifflin, c. 1964. Unpaged. (2-5)

          From his mountain home, a wise old farmer sees a tidal wave
          coming and warns the people in the village below by setting
          fire to his precious rice fields. Well-told adaptation of
          the original tale, but the illustrations contain so many
          Chinese elements that are presented as Japanese that these
          errors detract from the quality of the work. The version as
          told by Sara Bryant (see The Burning Rice Fields) is better.

6-026.   Ishii, Momoko. Issun Boshi, the Inchling: An Old Tale of
          Japan. Translated by Yone Mizuta. Illustrated by Fuku
          Akino. New York: Walker, c. 1967. Unpaged. (K-3)

          A childless couple pray to the sun for a child and get a boy
          who is no bigger than a person's thumb. They name him Issun
          Boshi, issun meaning "one inch." Issun Boshi makes his way
          to the capital by sailing the river to find a fortune and
          serves his mistress, the beautiful daughter of an
          aristocrat, faithfully. He saves her life from an attack by
          ogres. By the power of a magic mallet the ogres have left
          behind, the inchling becomes a tall, handsome, young man and
          marries his mistress. Although the style of the translation
          is not very good, splendid illustrations, which are like a
          picture scroll, give a fascinating effect to this story.
          Children will be fascinated by the beauty of the book.

6-027.   Iwaya Sazanami's Japanese Fairy Tales. Translated by Tsuda,
          Umeko and Hannah Riddle. Edited by Hokuseido. Tokyo:
          Hokuseido Press, 1951. 178 p. (2-6)

          In 1938, Hokuseido Press published twelve volumes of
          folktales retold by Iwaya. The stories in this book are six
          of the most well-told and are accompanied by detailed
          black-and-white illustrations.

6-028.   James, Grace. Green Willow and Other Japanese Fairy Tales.

See Japanese Fairy Tales (1979)

6-029.   --------------. Japanese Fairy Tales. Facsimile Classics
Series. Illustrated by Warwick Goble. New York: Mayflower
Books, 1979. viii, 232 p. (7 up)

This collection of thirty Japanese legends, myths, and tales
was originally published in 1910 as Green Willow and Other
Japanese Fairy Tales. The translation closely follows the
original stories and is very accurate. It contains only a
few minor misspellings of Japanese words such as Ichizen
instead of Echizen and Tomodata instead of Tomotada. A very
charming book.

6-030.   Jameson, Cynthia. One for the Price of Two. Illustrated by
Anita Lobel. New York: Parents Magazine Press, Unpaged.
(3-6)

A bragging farmer learns a lesson from a clogmaker's
apprentice. All the people in the illustrations have Western
faces, and the names and words are often distorted and not
Japanese. The hairstyles and clothing of the people are not
authentic. Strange words such as "AiYie!" pop up in the
text, but the story itself is enjoyable.

6-031.   The Japan Times. Publication Department. Folk Tales of Old
Japan. Sumie illustrations by Mitsuo Shirane. Tokyo: The
Japan Times, c. 1975. 119 p. (K-6)

This is a collection of sixteen famous folktales which have
been told in Japan generation after generation. Most of the
stories are reproduced from a series titled "Folk Tales of
Old Japan" which was published in the Information Bulletin
of the Public Information Bureau, Ministry of Foreign
Affairs of Japan between 1971 and 1972. At the end of the
book, there is a short background note for each tale. It is
disappointing that in these tales which appeared in a
Japanese government publication the details of some tales
have been changed from the widely-known version.

6-032.   Japanese Fairy Tales. Great Golden Book. Translated by
Mildred Murmur. Illustrated by Ben Venuti. New York:
Golden Press, c. 1960. 66 p. (K-2)

The book claims these stories are translated from Japanese
fairy tales, but they are free adaptations and not straight
translations. Some words are misspelled. The illustrations
are not authentic and often are a stereo-typed mixture of
Chinese and Japanese.

6-033. <u>Japanese Fairy Tales by Lafcadio Hearn and Others</u>. Great
    Neck: New York: Core Collection Books, 1979. 160 p. (4-9)

    A collection of twenty fairy tales retold by early American
    scholars of Japan. All the stories are authentic and well
    written. The print is large and easy to read; there are no
    illustrations. Half of the stories are difficult to find
    elsewhere, which makes this reprint edition especially
    valuable.

6-034. Kanzawa, Toshiko. <u>Raintaro</u>. Illustrated by Daihachi Ohta.
    Translated by Ann Herring. Tokyo: Gakken, c. 1972. 23 p.
    (K-2)

    A story of a crybaby who is nicknamed Raintaro (Rain Boy) by
    other children because he cries so much. One summer his
    village suffers drought. The boy's grandmother, who actually
    had found him crying on the street and brought him home to
    raise, becomes ill because of the lack of water. Raintaro
    starts off to get some water from the Milky Way. He climbs
    up to the very top of the tall cedar tree in the village to
    reach the sky but finds that it is not tall enough. He calls
    to the heaven for help and then is taken to heaven.
    Meanwhile, water from the Milky Way is delivered to the sick
    old woman, and all the villagers are overjoyed to see
    pouring rain. But from that time on, nobody ever sees that
    crybaby, Raintaro, again. Very effective and authentic
    illustrations.

6-035. Kishi, Nami. <u>The Ogre and His Bride</u>. Pictures by Shosuke
    Fukuda. English version by Alvin Tresselt. New York:
    Parents' Magazine Press, c. 1971. Unpaged. (K-2)

    Translation of <u>Oni no Yomesan</u> published by Kaiseisha in
    1969. The story of a lonely, ugly ogre who is looking for a
    bride. In exchange for rain which was badly needed in the
    village, a farmer offered one of his daughters to the ogre.
    The ogre made it rain, but the farmer's wife outwitted the
    simple-minded ogre and saved their daughter. The story is
    based on the custom that on the day before the calendrical
    beginning of spring, every Japanese household scatters
    parched soy beans to drive evil spirits from the house
    saying, "Devil stay outside! Happiness stay inside!" Very
    attractively illustrated to match the mood of the text, and
    the translation is superb.

6-036. Kume, Gen'ichi. <u>Kintaro's Adventure: Picture Plays for
    Kindergarten, School, Home</u>. Illustrated by Jyu Nonoguchi.
    Rutland, VT: Tuttle, c. 1964. 20 panels. (K-4)

Story of Kintaro, the legendary Japanese boy who was brought
up among animals in the mountains and was strong enough to
beat the bears in wrestling. Illustrations are authentic,
but it is regrettable that the reteller made many
unnecessary changes in the story. To be read and shown to
the class.

6-037.   Lifton, Betty Jean. The Mud Snail Son. Illustrated by Fuku
          Akino. New York: Atheneum, c. 1971. 38 p. (K-3)

An old couple living in a Japanese village want a child so
badly that they pray to the god of water to give them any
kind of baby so long as it would be their own. One evening
the wife gives birth to a tanishi, a mud snail. The couple
take good care of it twenty long years until they become too
old to work. The mud snail takes over and does all the work
for the old parents. He even marries a wealthy man's
daughter. Through his wife's love, devotion, and prayer, the
mud snail one day becomes a handsome young man. The story is
well-told and retains all the flavor of the original
folktale. Fuku Akino, who does many of the illustrations for
Lifton's works, alternates black-and-white and color
illustrations with absolutely beautiful and authentic
watercolor. Excellent book to explain Japanese culture and
values to young children.

6-038.   McAlpine, Helen and McAlpine, William. Japanese Tales and
          Legends. Oxford Myths and Legends. Illustrated by Joan
          Kiddell-Monroe. New York: Walck, c. 1959. 212 p. (5 up)

The legends and myths of Japan, including the birth of
Japan. This collection includes Japanese myths and stories
not found in other collections. Generally speaking, both
text and illustrations are good. The traditional folktales,
fairy tales, and myths are told in a readable style.

6-039.   McDermott, Gerald. The Stone-Cutter: A Japanese Folk Tale.
          Adapted and illustrated by Gerald McDermott. New York:
          Viking, c. 1975. Unpaged. (K-3)

Tasaku, a stone-cutter who has been content with his work,
sees a magnificent procession one day. His wish to become a
prince starts with the procession and is granted by the
mountain spirit. His wish escalates until finally he
realizes how foolish he was to long for power. A powerful
Japanese fable both in illustrations and theme of the text.
Illustrations match the message of the text perfectly. The
author shows a reasonable grasp of Japanese culture. The
text is well-written. It could be read to a small group, and
is also available in filmstrips.

6-040.   Matsui, Tadashi. <u>Oniroku and the Carpenter</u>. Illustrated by
          Suekichi Akaba. Translated from the Japanese by Masako
          Matsuno. Englewood Cliffs, NJ: Prentice-Hall, c. 1963.
          Unpaged. (K-3)

          A carpenter is asked to build a bridge across a very swift
          river. An ogre who lives in the river promises to do the
          difficult task of building the bridge in exchange for the
          carpenter's eyes. If the carpenter manages to guess the
          ogre's name (Oniroku), he will be able to save his eyes. The
          carpenter comes across a group of children singing about the
          ogre and his name and saves his eyes. A Japanese folktale
          similar to that of Rumplestiltskin in theme. Attractive and
          vivid illustrations and a well-translated text should
          attract readers.

6-041.   Matsuno, Masako. <u>Taro and the Bamboo Shoot: A Japanese Tale</u>.
          Illustrated by Yasuo Segawa. Adapted from the Japanese by
          Alice Low. New York: Knopf/Pantheon, 1974. Unpaged. (K-3)

          A tall tale of a Japanese village boy who climbs on a fast
          growing bamboo and of villagers who live far from the sea.
          Taro, a Japanese boy, goes to dig a bamboo shoot for dinner
          for his birthday and gets on a fast-growing bamboo by
          mistake. When the boy's father and relatives cut off the
          bamboo to save the boy's life, the bamboo becomes a road to
          lead the people of the village to the sea none of them have
          ever seen. Fairly well-told, entertaining story, but there
          is one mistake--traditionally, Japanese never celebrated
          birthdays. Authentic but humorous illustrations in
          alternating black-and-white and color are very effectively
          used.

6-042.   Matsutani, Miyoko. <u>The Crane Maiden</u>. Illustrated by Chihiro
          Iwasaki. English version by Alvin Tresselt. New York:
          Parents' Magazine Press, c. 1968. Unpaged. (K-3)

          Another version of a popular Japanese folktale (see Bartoli,
          <u>The Story of the Grateful Crane</u>). The illustrations are
          absolutely lovely. There are two mistakes in the text. In
          the translation the girl says, "My name is Tsuru-san," which
          no Japanese would say since the honorific <u>san</u> is never used
          in speaking of oneself. The second error concerns the custom
          of kissing. The text reads: "She (the crane) kissed the man
          and his wife tenderly." In this particular situation,
          Japanese do not kiss each other; they bow. Japanese do not
          kiss in public.

6-043.   ----------------. <u>The Fisherman Under the Sea</u>. Illustrated by
          Chihiro Iwasaki. English version by Alvin Tresselt. New
          York: Parents' Magazine Press, c. 1969. Unpaged. (K-4)

This is an old Japanese tale of Urashima Taro, a fisherman. One day, Urashima rescues a turtle and the turtle takes him to a palace under the sea. He has a good time day after day, but one day he wants to go home. As he is leaving the palace, he is given a box and told never to open it. When he comes back to his old village, everything has changed. He realizes that he has become a complete stranger. In despair he opens the box and in an instant he becomes an old man. Beautifully told Japanese folktale with a sad ending. The text is well-written, and the pastel illustrations are exquisite.

6-044.   ----------------. The Fox Wedding. Illustrated by Yasuo Segawa. Translated by Masako Matsuno. Chicago: Encyclopedia Britannica, c. 1963. Unpaged. (1-4)

An old man raises an abandoned baby fox until it grew into a beautiful female fox. It disappears one day and the old man sees a fox wedding procession crossing the rainbow. This story is based on the legend that when it rains and the sun shines at the same time a fox wedding is taking place. The illustrations are done in pastel rainbow colors. A little, sad story, but is a beautifully made picture book.

6-045.   ----------------. Gengoroh and the Thunder God. Illustrated by Yasuo Segawa. New York: Parents' magazine Press, 1970. Unpaged. (K-3)

Gengoroh, a handsome, carefree, but very poor young man, is out strolling and finds a small magic drum. By beating on the drum and saying magic words, he can make people's noses grow long or short. He uses the power of the drum to trick people and becomes rich. But after awhile, he is bored and decides to see how long his own nose can grow. His nose grows and grows until it reaches heaven. It so happens that a carpenter in heaven is building a bridge and uses the end of the nose as one of the poles of the bridge. When Gengoroh says the magic words to shorten his nose, he is lifted to heaven because his nose is secured to the bridge. In heaven, he becomes a helper of the thunder god. One day, he slips off the side of a cloud and falls into a large lake on earth. He still lives there as Gengoroh carp. A funny and entertaining tall tale. The effective and creative use of illustrations brings the story to life. Could be used for individual reading or for reading to a group. Highly recommended.

6-046.   ----------------. How the Withered Trees Blossomed. Pictures by Yasuo Segawa. Philadelphia: Lippincott, 1971. 40 p. (K-3)

An old Japanese folktale of how Hanasakajijii, a good-
natured old man who loves his white dog dearly, becomes
rich. He is able to make withered trees blossom with the
ashes made from a willow tree that grows where his dog is
buried after his wicked neighbor killed the dog. This book
opens from the back, and is printed and bound in Japanese
style. It includes texts in both English and Japanese.
Attractive, colorful illustrations by Yasuo Segawa are a
good contribution to the usefulness and quality of this
book, especially for American classrooms.

6-047.   ----------------. Taro, the Dragon-Boy. Translation by Donald
          C. Boone. Illustrations by Masakazu Kuwata. Palo Alto, CA:
          Kodansha International, 1967. 127 p. (3-6)

Translation of Tatsunoko Taro which was based on a
traditional legend. A Japanese woman who was inconsiderate
to others was turned into a dragon. With the help of her
son, Taro, the Dragon Boy, his friend Aya, a red ogre, and
thunder gods, the dragon destroys a mountain so that the
lake dammed by the mountain becomes a river. The new river
provides water for new rice fields whose harvest eases the
hunger of the people. This good deed and Taro's tears change
the dragon back into human form. A good story.

6-048.   ----------------. The Witch's Magic Cloth. English version by
          Alvin Tresselt. Illustrated by Yasuo Segawa. New York:
          Parents' Magazine Press, 1969. 32 p. (K-2)

The witch of the mountain commands the villagers to bring
rice cakes as an offering because she has just given birth
to a baby boy. An old woman is chosen to bring them to the
witch. Because of the old woman's courage and hard work, the
old woman is given a magic roll of cloth which will never be
used up. Very good translation retaining all the flavor of
the original tale. Humorous and colorful illustrations.

6-049.   Men from the Village Deep in the Mountains: And Other
          Japanese Folk Tales. Translated and illustrated by Garrett
          Bang. New York: Macmillan, c. 1973. 84 p. (2-6)

Twelve intriguing folktales translated from authoritative
Japanese folklore collections. The source on which the
translations are based is cited. There is only one mistake
in the text. It reads, "she stood up from the chair," when
in the illustration she is sitting on the floor. In
traditional Japan there were no chairs; people sat on the
floor. Except for that one mistake, both text and
illustrations are very good.

6-050.   Mitford, A.B. Tales of Old Japan. Rutland, VT: Tuttle, 1966.
          383 p. (5 up)

This is one of the earliest anthologies of Japanese tales to appear in English. It was originally published in London in 1871 and then in New York by Macmillan in 1893. The collection contains folktales, historical legends, ghost stories, and Buddhist sermons. Also included are essays explaining some aspects of Japanese culture. Many of the stories are not found in other English collections. The woodblock illustrations were made specifically for this book and were cut by a famous nineteenth-century Tokyo wood engraver. The stories are translated well. Footnotes.

6-051.   Morsel, Arlene, The Funny Little Woman. Pictures by Blair Lent. New York: Dutton, c. 1972. Unpaged. (K-2)

This story tells of a woman who likes to make dumplings and laugh strange laughs. One day, while she is chasing a dumpling she has dropped, she is captured by ogres because she cannot help laughing. While she is in captivity she cooks rice day after day for the ogres with a magic paddle. One day when the ogres are gone, she manages to escape with the magic paddle. After her safe return home she becomes a prosperous rice dumpling maker because of the magic paddle. This book was awarded the Caldecott Medal in 1972, but there are several illustrative and textual mistakes. Besides, this author does not seem to know what a rice dumpling is. Japanese rice dumplings are made from rice flour, not from cooked rice. This story was originally introduced by Lafcadio Hearn whose translation is still preferred.

6-052.   Naito, Hiroshi. Legends of Japan. Retold by Hiroshi Naito, and illustrated by Masahiko Nishino. Rutland, VT: Tuttle, c. 1972. 111 p. (3-7)

Twenty-two very short legends are included. The stories were taken from the Konjaku Monogatari, a famous collection of old Japanese legends and stories written over a thousand years ago, and originally published in the Mainichi Daily News. The stories are well-selected and well-translated.

6-053.   Newman, Shirlee P. Folk Tales of Japan. Folk Tales Around the World Series. Adapted by Shirlee P. Newman. Editorial consultant: Jeanne Chall. Drawings by Emilio Freixas and Thomas Culver. Indianapolis: Bobbs-Merrill, c. 1963. 111 p. (3-9)

The stories are called adaptations, but they are actually a rewriting of the folktales with very little change from the originals. The rewriting was carefully done to make the stories interesting and readable. Some of the names are misspelled. The illustrations are detailed, but

unfortunately they are a mixture of Chinese and Japanese
elements and not authentic. These would be particularly good
stories to read to children.

6-054.   Newton, Patricia Montogomery. The Five Sparrows: A Japanese
Folktale. New York: Atheneum, 1982. Unpaged. (1-4)

This story is adapted from the Uji Shui Monogatari (Tales
from the Uji Collection), a thirteenth-century collection. A
kind old woman rescues a sparrow with a broken back and
nurses it back to health, despite the teasing of the people
around her. When the wound is healed, the old woman frees
the sparrow. The sparrow returns a few days later and brings
a gourd seed. The woman plants the seed and tends it
carefully. When harvest time comes, she has more gourds than
she can use, so she shares them with everyone in the
village. She dries the leftover gourds and they bring her
family wealth. A greedy neighbor, envious of the woman,
looks for an injured sparrow to tend; and when she cannot
find any, she injures some sparrows herself. Because the
neighbor had more sparrows, she thought her reward would be
greater; but there was no reward for her at all. Well-told
story with good illustrations.

6-055.   O'Donnell, James E. Japanese Folk Tales. Illustrated by
Kasumi Nagao. Caldwell, ID: The Caxton Printers, 1958. 92
p. (2-6)

Eight famous folktales are included in this book. The
reteller talked to many older men and women in Japan and
pieced together the stories in this book." The stories are
accurate and told in clear English. In the original stories,
the characters seldom had names but the reteller assigned
them Japanese names, which was not necessary. The stories
are accompanied by many authentic, full-color illustrations.
There are a few mistakes. On page 50, children are said to
kiss the parents. In Japan, kissing was not done as a way of
salutation. On p. 52, it is said that a sparrow hid itself
under a chair. Chairs were non-existent in old Japan.

6-056.   O-E Yama: The Story of General Raiko and the Ogres of O-E
Yama. Drawings by Suiho Yanai. Tokyo: Fuji Publishing, c.
1959. Unpaged. (K-2)

A picture story book of an old Japanese legend about the
Ogres of O-E Mountain (near Kyoto) and a brave samurai.
Giant ogres appeared at the Great Gate of Rashomon in Kyoto
night after night to attack the people and carry off the
women and children to their mountain stronghold. General
Raiko sent one of his strongest retainers to take care of
the situation. The retainer cut off an arm of one of the
ogres who appeared in the form of a beautiful woman. Raiko

and his men then went to O-E Mountains disguised as
wandering pilgrims. With the help of a magic potion of wine
given to them by a mountain hermit, Raiko and his men were
able to rescue all the prisoners and retrieve the treasure.
All illustrations are in color and are very detailed and
authentic.

6-057.   Ozaki, Yei Theodora. Japanese Fairy Books. Illustrated by F.
          Fujiyama. New York: Dover, 1967. Paperback edition by
          Tuttle, 1970, 292 p. (3-6)

First published in 1903, with a second edition in 1922, and
the latest a 1970 paperback from Tuttle, this collection of
twenty-two Japanese fairy tales includes many stories not
available in other collections. The style is a little old-
fashioned, but it is an accurate translation with authentic
illustrations by a Japanese artist. Very good and still
useful in the classroom as well as for individual reading.

6-058.   Piggott, Juliet. Fairy Tales of Japan. Illustrated by
          Jennifer Druy Harris. New York: Dutton, c. 1961. Unpaged.
          (3-6)

Three well-known Japanese folktales are retold in this book.
The reteller changed the original tales to a great extent
and in a way which does not seem to serve any purpose. The
illustrations are bad; they are a stereotyped mixture of
pseudo-Japanese style and they incorrectly combine clothing,
accessories, and foot-gear styles.

6-059.   ----------------. Japanese Fairy Tales. The World Fairy Tale
          Collections. Illustrated by Harry Toothill. Chicago:
          Follett, 1967. 198 p. (3-8)

First published in London in 1962, this is a collection of
thirteen Japanese folktales and myths which the author was
told as a child growing up in Japan or which were drawn from
her study of Japanese folklore. There are fewer mistakes in
this than in similar works, but there are still a few.
Prince Yamamoto should be Prince Yamato, and men and boys do
not exclaim "Maa," because it is a word used only by women.

6-060.   --------------. Japanese Mythology. New York: Hamlyn, c.
          1969. 141 p. (9 up)

This book includes many legends and folktales as well as
myths. The stories are grouped by type or topic. Included
are tales about supernatural beings and animals, legends of
heroes and heroines, and creation myths. Explanation and
background are given for the tales. Abundantly illustrated

primarily with reproductions of <u>ukiyoe</u> prints and
photographs. Unfortunately, there are several mistakes in
romanization, most in the description of the illustrations.

6-061.   Porter, Wesley. <u>The Magic Kettle: Japanese Folk Legend</u>.
Retold by Wesley Porter. Illustrated by Lynn Sweat. New
York: Watts, 1979. 27 p. (K-3)

This is a strange retelling of a Japanese folktale. The
story itself is not told well and the reteller changed the
original story a great deal. The illustrations are a mixture
of Chinese, Japanese, and American styles. The <u>hibachi</u> in
the illustrations is an American barbecue grill, not a
Japanese <u>hibachi</u>. Not recommended.

6-062.   Pratt, Davis and Elsa Kula. <u>Magic Animals of Japan</u>.
Berkeley, CA: Parnassus, 1967. Unpaged. (2-6)

A collection of Japanese folklore in which animals play
important roles. The stories explain the traits which the
Japanese connect with certain animals. It is a very
informative and well-organized book. When the class is
studying about "animals as friends," this would be the right
book to use in connection with another culture. The animals
included are real, legendary, and mythical.

6-063.   <u>The Rabbit Who Lost His Fur: A Favorite Story from Japan</u>.
English version by Ralph Friedrich. Illustrations by
Toshio Suzuki. Rutland, VT: Tuttle, 1960. Unpaged. (K-1)

This story appears in the <u>Kojiki</u>, one of the first two
chronicles of Japanese history written (ca. 700 A.D.). A
white rabbit, living on an island, wants to go to the
mainland. He challenges a shark to compare the number of
friends each has. He has the shark call his friends and then
has the sharks line up from his island to the mainland so he
can count them. The rabbit crosses over the sharks to the
mainland, and as soon as he lands, he mocks the sharks. The
angry sharks whisk off all the rabbit's fur. The rabbit is
in severe pain, and when a troup of chieftains pass by, they
tell the rabbit the best thing to do is to bathe in the sea
and dry himself in the wind, which only makes the pain
worse. Another passing chieftain teaches the rabbit how to
get well. The morale of the story is quite clear—cheating
is punished and kindness appreciated.

6-064.   Sakade, Florence. <u>Japanese Children's Favorite Stories</u>.
Illustrated by Yoshisuke Kurosaki. Rutland, VT: Tuttle, c.
1958. 120 p. (1-4)

This revised edition of a well-known collection of stories
contains twenty folktales. Most of the translations are true
to the original tales, but it is regrettable that some
unnecessary changes were made in some of the stories. The
illustrations were done by a well-known Japanese illustrator
of children's books, and they clearly depict how people
dress and how places look. They will provide an authentic
picture of Japan for young readers.

6-065.   ---------------. Japanese Children's Stories. Illustrated by
         Yoshio Hayashi. Rutland, VT: Tuttle, c. 1959. 120 p. (1-4)

This is a companion volume to Japanese Children's Favorite
Stories. This volume contains eighteen stories, most of them
folktales but some of them by modern Japanese authors of
children's literature. The stories were selected from Gin no
Suzu (Silver Bells), a famous children's magazine. Many of
the folktales are unnecessarily changed from the original.
Illustrations are done very well and accurately depict
Japanese scenes.

6-066.   ---------------. ed. Little One-Inch and Other Japanese
         Children's Favorite Stories. Illustrated by Yoshisuke
         Kurosaki. Rutland, VT: Tuttle, c. 1958. 60 p. (1-4)

Includes ten short stories. This is the paperback version of
the two Sakade volumes listed above.

6-067.   ---------------. ed. Peach Boy: And Other Japanese
         Children's Favorite Stories. Illustrated by Yoshisuke
         Kurosaki. Rutland, VT: Tuttle, c. 1958. 1972 printing. 58
         p. (1-4)

This is a reprint of the first nine stories in Japanese
Children's Favorite Stories by Sakade.

6-068.   ---------------. ed. Urashima Taro and Other Japanese
         Children's Stories. Illustrated by Yoshio Hayashi.
         Rutland, VT: Tuttle, 1964, 1976 printing. 57 p. (1-4)

This is the reprint of the first ten stories from Sakade's
Japanese Children's Stories.

6-069.   Samuel, Yoshiko. Twelve Years, Twelve Animals: A Japanese
         Folk Tale. Adapted by Yoshiko Samuel. Illustrated by Margo
         Lock. New York: Abingdon, c. 1972. Unpaged. (K-3)

A story to explain how the years got their names in Japan
and why cats and mice do not get along to this day. The
illustrations are a bad mixture of Chinese and Japanese
elements. There is a calendar of animal names for the years
at the end of the book in which readers can find their birth

year. Actually, the cycle of twelve years with the names of
animals started in China, not in Japan. So in that sense
also, this book is misleading.

6-070.   Say, Allen. Once Upon the Cherry Blossom Tree: An Old
         Japanese Tale. Retold and illustrated by Allen Say. New
         York: Harper & Row, c. 1974. 31 p. (K-4)

A miserly old landlord lives in a small village in Japan. He
is mean and greedy and makes all the villagers suffer by
collecting too much rent for the land. He complains, too.
One day, he swallows a cherry pit and it grows into a cherry
tree which sprouts from the top of his head. People ridicule
him, and out of rage the miserly landlord pulls it out of
his head. The hole left when he pulled out the tree is
filled with water, and eventually fish start to live in it.
Children have a good time fishing in the hole whenever the
man takes a nap. One day, when the landlord finds out what
the children have been doing, he chases them away, stumbles,
and disappears. All that is left of the wicked landlord is a
lovely lake. Well-told, funny, tall tale. Good illustrations
to match the mood of the story by the reteller of the story
himself.

6-071.   Scofield, Elizabeth. A Fox in One Bite: And Other Tasty
         Tales from Japan. Illustrated by K. Wakana. Tokyo:
         Kodansha International, c. 1965. 44 p. (K-4)

Six tales about foxes and badgers are told in this well-
illustrated and well-written short book. Suitable for
individual reading and reading to a group. Each tale has one
color and one black-and-white illustration. The use of much
Japanese onomatopoeia is effective.

6-072.   ----------------. Hold Tight, Stick Tight. Illustrations by
         K. Wakana. Tokyo: Kodansha International, c. 1966. 46 p.
         (1-6)

An accurate, enjoyable collection of Japanese folktales,
well selected and well-told. In each of the tales in this
collection there is an honest, hard-working old man who is
rewarded for his goodness and a wicked old neighbor who
imitates his good neighbor to get his share of good fortune,
but who ends up in disaster--the kind of reward he deserves
for his greediness. Authentic and humorous illustrations
contribute a great deal to the book.

6-073.   Seki, Keigo. Folktales of Japan. Folktales of the World.
         Translated by Robert J. Adams. Chicago: University of
         Chicago Press, c. 1963. xxi, 221 p. (10 up)

Although this translation was mainly done for the purpose of
academic study, this collection of Japanese folktales can be
used for reading for entertainment. The book is divided into
six sections by theme: animal tales; ogres; supernatural
husbands and wives; kindness rewarded and evil punished;
good fortune; and cleverness and stupidity. All the tales
translated here were chosen from a compilation by Keigo
Seki, a noted Japanese folklorist and a disciple of the
founder of the scientific study of folklore in Japan, Kunio
Yanagita. Seki selected some sixty three common tales from a
total of over 15,000 tales collected throughout Japan for
his Nihon no Mukashibanashi (Japanese folktales). The
translations are very readable. At the beginning of each
tale, the type of the tale, the motif, and the translator's
note are given. Appended with a good glossary, a
bibliography, and an index.

6-074.   Stamm, Claus. Dumpling and the Demons. Illustrated by Kazue
         Mizumura. New York: Viking, c. 1964. 44 p. (K-3)

An old man follows a talking dumpling into a cave where he
finds a statue of Jizo, the god of children, and outwits the
demons who are gambling there. The old man's sneaky neighbor
tries the same thing, but fails miserably because he
completely lacks consideration and respect. Comical
illustrations complement the text well for a better
understanding of Japanese culture.

6-075.   ----------------. Three Strong Women: A Tall Tale from Japan.
         Illustrated by Kazue Mizumura. New York: Viking, c. 1962.
         47 p. (1-5)

A humorous tall tale from Japan about three strong women and
a sumo wrestler. A self-contained sumo wrestler meets a
little girl on his way to the capital for a match. He
follows her to her home and becomes extremely strong after
practicing with these three women. He defeats all the other
contestants in the capital and comes back to these women to
live with them. The four of them are still practicing to
this day, and that is why we still hear an occasional
earthshaking sound from the mountains of Japan. Kazue
Mizumura's illustrations match the humorous atmosphere of
this tale and add the finishing touch. Children will have a
good time listening to or reading this unusual tall tale.

6-076.   ----------------. The Very Special Badgers: A Tale of Magic
         from Japan. Illustrated by Kazue Mizumura. New York:
         Viking. 1960. 40 p. (1-5)

A funny story of a battle of wits between two rival tribes
of tanuki, a kind of badger, on neighboring islands in old
Japan. The agreement of the two tribes is that each group

will send the best in the tribe to a cheat-and-change
contest, and whichever side loses has to go to a faraway
place forever. Both text and illustrations are good and
accurate. Tanukis have an important role in Japanese
folklore because they are believed to have the magical power
to change into whatever they wish to be.

6-077.   Steinberg, Barbara Hope. The Magic Millstones and Other
          Japanese Folk Stories. Illustrated by Esme Eve. Oxford:
          Oxford University Press, 1969. 64 p. (5 up)

          Includes nine well-known Japanese folktales. Text is told
          with some adaptation but is still all right. However, the
          illustrations are badly influenced by stereotyped Japanese
          woodblock prints and are full of mistakes.

6-078.   Suzuki, Yoshimatsu. Japanese Legends and Folk-Tales. Tokyo:
          Sakurai Shoten, 1951. 144 p. (6 up)

          This compilation was originally done for use by Japanese
          students studying English. Forty-three very short stories
          and folktales, which are not found in other collections, are
          included. No illustrations.

6-079.   Tabra, Ruth. ed. Momotaro: Peach Boy. An Island Heritage
          Book. Adapted from the original folktales by Island
          Heritage. Illustrated by George Suyeoka. New York:
          Weatherhill, c. 1972. Unpaged. (2-5)

          Authentic, beautiful, detailed, and powerful full-color
          illustrations makes this edition of a famous Japanese
          folktale highly recommended. Accompanied with a good,
          readable, text. At the end of the book detailed pictures and
          explanations of the Japanese things which appeared in the
          story are included.

6-080.   Titus, Eve. The Two Stonecutters. Illustrated by Yoko
          Mitsuhashi. New York: Doubleday, c. 1967. Unpaged. (K-5)

          A well-told adaptation of a Japanese folktale with strong
          moral teaching about two brothers who make their living as
          stonecutters. These brothers were granted seven wishes by
          the Goddess of the Forest in return for their kindness to
          her. Clear, powerful, and authentic illustrations. Highly
          recommended.

6-081.   Uchida, Yoshiko. The Dancing Kettle: And Other Japanese Folk
          Tales. Illustrated by Richard C. Jones. New York:
          Harcourt, Brace, c. 1949. 174 p. (3-5)

This collection of Japanese folktales is well-known to
school librarians and teachers in this country. Uchida
states in the preface, "I have retold them in my own words,
and have taken the liberty of adapting them so they would be
more meaningful to the children of America." The reteller
makes too many unnecessary changes in her effort to make
things easier for American children, and by making the
changes, she almost distorts the original stories. For
example, an ogre is changed to a ghost, and the
illustrations show Western ghosts. The illustrations are
especially bad because of the mixture of Chinese and
Japanese elements. The reteller has almost done a disservice
to the readers.

6-082.   ----------------. The Magic Listening Cap: More Folk Tales
          from Japan. Retold and illustrated by Yoshiko Uchida. New
          York: Harcourt, c. 1955. 146 p. (4-6)

Fourteen Japanese folk tales are retold in this collection.
Some of the tales are retold in a straightforward manner,
and there are fewer changes of the original tales in this
collection than in her first collection of Japanese
folktales. Uchida did the black-and-white illustrations
herself. In the preface Uchida stresses what folktales can
do in increasing understanding in the children of the world,
thus it is regrettable that she still changed the details of
the original tale. A glossary is included.

6-083.   ----------------. The Sea of Gold, and Other Tales from
          Japan. Adapted by Yoshiko Uchida. Illustrated by Marianne
          Yamaguchi. New York: Scribner, c. 1965. 136 p. (3-6)

Twelve Japanese folktales are adapted and included in this
collection. The original stories are somewhat less changed
than in her former collection, The Dancing Kettle. The
changes are regrettable because many do not seem necessary
and the tales do not benefit from the changes. The
illustrations are not very good. Glossary.

6-084.   Ury, Marian. Tales of Times Now Past: Sixty-Two Stories from
          a Medieval Japanese Collection. Berkeley; University of
          Califronia Press, c. 1979. xi 199 p. (10 up)

These stories were taken from the Konjaku Monogatarishu, a
collection of over 1000 brief tales from medieval Japan.
There is an extensive introduction at the beginning of the
book and each story is accompanied by explanatory notes. The
collection includes stories originally from India and China
as well as Japan. Stories from Japan comprise about 60 per
cent of the collection. Many stories have a strong religious
tone. Selected bibliography of the texts and translations of
the Konjaki Monogatarishu are also included.

6-085. Van Woerkom, Dorothy O. <u>Sea Frog, City Frog: Adapted from A</u>
        <u>Japanese Folk Tale</u>. Ready-to-Read Book. Pictures by Jose
        Aruego and Ariane Dewey. New York: Macmillan, c. 1975.
        Unpaged. (K-2)

        A truly enjoyable picture book adapted from a Japanese
        folktale. The story has been simplified, is funny, and has a
        clear moral. The illustrations are very well-done but are
        completely Western.

6-086. Wakana, Kei. <u>The Magic Hat</u>. New York: Scroll Press, c. 1970.
        Unpaged. (K-3)

        By putting on a magic cap, a man can understand what
        nonhumans are talking about. A good story with humorous,
        authentic illustrations. This is a bilingual story which is
        printed in Japanese style, opening from the back. Enjoyable
        and educational. <u>The Magic Listening Cap</u> by Yoshiko Uchida
        is the same story.

6-087. Wheeler, Post. <u>Tales from the Japanese Storytellers, as</u>
        <u>Collected in the Ho-Dan-Zo</u>. Selected and edited by Harold
        G. Henderson. Rutland, VT: Tuttle, 1976. 139 p. (10 up)

        These twenty-four stories are selected from the ten-volume
        collection of stories taken from public storytellers and
        compiled by Wheeler. The collection includes a variety of
        stories from the Edo period and the tales reveal much about
        Japanese culture and customs. The first edition was
        published by Weatherhill in 1964. The Tuttle edition is in
        paperback. A glossary is included.

6-088. Yagawa, Sumiko. <u>The Crane Wife</u>. Translation from the
        Japanese by Katherine Paterson. Illustrated by Suekichi
        Akaba. New York: William Morrow, 1981. Unpaged. (K-4)

        A good translation of a well-known old Japanese folktale. A
        poor young farmer saves a wounded crane and the grateful
        crane returns as a beautiful young woman who becomes his
        wife. In order to make ends meet, the wife volunteers to
        weave but only on the condition that her husband never look
        at her while she is weaving. She weaves exquisite silk cloth
        and Yohei, the husband, sells it for a high price in town.
        When the money is gone, she volunteers to weave the cloth
        one more time only. Each time she weaves, she becomes
        exhausted and thinner. A greedy neighbor, hoping to make a
        fortune by selling cloth in the capital, convinces the
        simple-minded farmer to make his wife weave one more time.
        She reluctantly agrees. After waiting days while his wife
        weaves, the husband's curiosity gets the best of him and he
        peeks into the room only to find out... The translator keeps
        the original Japanese onomatopoeia, and it adds a rhythmic

effect when read aloud. The illustrations are breathtakingly
beautiful and catch the mood of the story perfectly. There
is a guide to the Japanese words in the text and their
pronunciation. A perfect book to read aloud to a small
group. Most highly recommended.

6-089.   Yamaguchi, Tohr. The Golden Crane: A Japanese Folk Tale.
          Illustrated by Marianne Yamaguchi. New York: Holt,
          Rinehart and Winston, c. 1963. 30 p. (3-5)

Toshi, a deaf-and-dumb boy who lost his father in a storm at
sea, comes to live with an old man in a small Japanese
fishing village. The boy finds a wounded golden crane one
day and nurses it to health. People come to know about it,
and the crane attracts much attention. Toshi and the old man
try to keep the crane, but the emperor, who is the most
powerful man in the country, orders them to give the crane
to him. In order to prevent this from happening, a
tremendous number of cranes appear and carry Toshi and the
old man away over the ocean with the wounded crane. There
are a few textual and illustrative mistakes. No poor
fisherman has silk cushions in his shack, and no Japanese
burns charcoal in a fireplace. Wood is used for fire.

6-090.   Yanagita, Kunio. Japanese Folk Tales: A Revised Selection.
          Translated by Fanny Hagin Mayer; illustrated by Kei
          Wakana. Tokyo: Tokyo News Service, 1966. 190 p. (3 up)

A collection of 106 short stores first published in 1954 and
revised in 1966. Good translations and illustrations. The
book includes an introduction, a reference index, a
geographical index, and a map showing the place of origin of
the tales.

6-091.   ----------------. The Legends of Tono. Translated, with an
          introduction by Ronald A. Morse. Tokyo: The Japan
          Foundation, 1975. xxxi, 90 p. (5 up)

This is the first work by the founder of Japanese ethnology.
It was published in Japanese in 1910 and corresponds to the
collection done by the Grimm Brothers. The legends were all
collected from a single storyteller from the village of
Tono, a mountain village with severe living conditions which
are reflected in the stories. Over 100 legends are recorded
and include a wide variety of legendary characters, such as
tengu, demons, goblins, monsters, animals, gods, and kappa.
Each tale is very short and some are similar to Western
legends. Maps and illustrations have been included in this
translation to help non-Japanese readers.

6-092.   Yashima, Taro. Seashore Story. Written and illustrated by T.
          Yashima. New York: Viking, c. 1967. Unpaged. (K-2)

This is an interpretation of the legend of Urashima Taro, the Japanese version of Rip Van Winkle. Vacationing Japanese ballet-school children listen to the old legend on a quiet seashore. Urashima, the fisherman, saves the life of a turtle and it takes him to a palace under the ocean. Urashima forgets about his family and the passing of time. When he comes home, he suddenly becomes an old man. All the children wonder about the meaning of the story. The haunting, abstract, but beautiful illustrations add to the mysterious mood. All readers will also wonder about the meaning of the story as the children in the story do.

6-093.   Yasuda, Yuri. Old Tales of Japan. Illustrated by Yoshinobu Sakurai and Eiichi Mitsui. 3rd revised ed. Rutland, VT: Tuttle, 1956, 1967 printing. 320 p. (1-4)

This collection contains twelve well-known and readable folktales of Japan and many authentic illustrations. The title for each tale is given both in English and Japanese.

6-094.   Yoda, Jun'ichi. The Rolling Rice Ball. illustrated by Saburo Watanabe. English version by Alvin Tresselt. New York: Parents' Magazine Press, c. 1969. Unpaged. (K-3)

A popular Japanese folktale. An old woodcutter is about to have his usual lunch of rice balls. He is hungry and in a hurry and he drops a rice ball to the ground where it rolls into a hole in the ground. The woodcutter thinks he hears a small voice from the hole. To satisfy his curiosity, he rolls all the rice balls into the hole one by one. A mouse comes out from the hole and invites the old man to the world of mice for his generosity. The mice give him a bamboo chest filled with gold coins as a souvenir. The woodcutter's neighbors overhear this story, and try to do the same. But because of their greedy and mean nature, things do not turn out the way they hope. This is translated into rather literary English, but it remains a humorous story. Comical and lively illustrations match the story.

6-095.   Zemach, Kaethe. The Beautiful Rat. Written and illustrated by the author. New York: Four Winds Press, c. 1979. Unpaged. (K-1)

This is a retelling of a well-known Japanese tale - although this is nowhere stated in the book. The proud rat parents of a beautiful rat daughter want her to marry a fine husband. The mother thinks her daughter is much too good to become the wife of a rat, while the daughter is perfectly happy with her rat friends. One day, the parents decide to offer their daughter to the sun because they think there is nothing greater than the sun. The sun tells them that the cloud is stronger than he is because the cloud can hide the

rays of the sun. The parents go to the cloud, and the cloud
says that the wind is stronger because it can blow him away.
When the rats talk with the wind, the wind says that the
stone wall is stronger. What the stone wall says is a good
surprise for all of them. The illustrations include many
Japanese things such as tea sets, fans, tables, etc., but
the clothing is inaccurate. In general, however, the
illustrations are lively and expressive and this makes up
for their inaccuracies.

7. SOCIAL STUDIES

GENERAL

7-001.   <u>American Japanese Coloring and Talking Books</u>. Rutland, VT:
         Tuttle, c. 1972. 10 v. (K-1)

According to the publisher, "Each book of this series (1.
Animals, 2. Holidays, 3. Eating, 4. Games, 5. Sightseeing,
6. Customs, 7. Dressing, 8. Riding, 9. Houses, 10. Storybook
heroes) is designed to serve both as a coloring book and as
a first step in international understanding--to introduce
the child to some of the differences in the ways and customs
of this country and Japan." The format varies slightly from
book to book; but generally, facing pages are devoted to one
topic, one page depicting something American, the other
something Japanese. Besides presenting pictures to color,
each page includes passages in English and Japanese to be
read aloud with each picture. The quality of the pictures
varies from book to book, depending on the artist, but
generally speaking this series could be used effectively in
the classroom or at home for an awareness of the differences
and similarities between the two cultures.

7-002.   Caldwell, John C. <u>Let's Visit Japan</u>, New York: Day, c. 1959,
         1965 printing. 96 p. (4-6)

The author uses what children already know about Japan as
his starting point to this introduction to Japan. Despite
its age, this book is a good overview of Japan and it is
better than some of the more recent works.

7-003.   Chamberlain, Basil Hall. Japanese Things: Being Notes on
         Various Subjects Connected with Japan. Rutland, VT:
         Tuttle, 1971. x, 568 p. (9 up)

This book was originally published by one of the first
western scholars of Japan at the end of the nineteenth
century under the title Things Japanese. The present edition
is a reprint of the fifth (1905) revised edition. Topics are
arranged in alphabetical order. Although this work is old,
it contains much of value especially as a historical record
of things which have since disappeared from Japanese culture
over the past seven decades.

7-004.   De Mente, Boye. The Whole Japan Book: An Encyclopedic Reader
         on Things Japanese. Phoenix, AZ: Phoenix Books, c. 1983.
         352 p. (10 up)

This book is designed to serve as an introduction to Japan
and to encourage further study. Approximately 800 words are
arranged in alphabetical order. If the entry word is in
English, the Japanese word is given with its pronunciation.
For many entries recommended readings are also given.
Illustrated with photographs and drawings. A list of
addresses for English-language sources is given at the end
of the book.

7-005.   Dolan, Edward, Jr. and Finney, Shan. The New Japan. New
         York: Watts, 1983, 118 p. (9-12)

The authors present a comprehensive view of Japan and its
people after 1945. The nine chapters cover the democratic
governmental system and politics, the miraculous industrial
development, schools, housing, the effects of modernization
on family life, the changing role of women, religions, and
recreation. Each concise chapter is further divided into
smaller, specific subjects. The text is accurately done and
easy to read. Romanization of Japanese words is mostly
accurate. The mistake found was on page 79, when the word
has to be sashimi, thin strips of raw fish, instead of
sushi. Appended with an index and a list of further reading
which includes many recent works.

7-006.   Forbis, William H. Japan Today: People, Places, Power. A
         Cass Canfield Book. Foreword by Mike Mansfield. New York:
         Harper & Row, c. 1975. 463 p. (10 up)

The author, a senior editor of Time Magazine, has produced a
vivid account of modern Japan. The book is organized in
three major sections. The section on people provides a good
introduction and insight into culture and society. The
section on places provides vivid word pictures of several
cities and rural areas. The section on power describes the

political and economic configuration of modern Japan. The
history of Japan is summarized in "Interludes" between the
sections.

7-007.   Hall, John Whitney and Beardsley, Richard K. <u>Twelve Doors to
          Japan</u>. New York: McGraw-Hill, c. 1965. xxi, 649 p. (10 up)

This is an excellent introductory volume on Japan. Each
chapter deals with one topic, such as language, art,
society, and is written by a specialist in that field for
people who know relatively little about Japan. Appended with
a general bibliography, selected bibliographies for each
chapter, and an extensive index.

7-008.   Japan Culture Institute. ed. <u>A Hundred Things Japanese</u>.
          Tokyo: The Japan Culture Institute, c. 1975. vi, 208 p.
          (10 up)

          Murakami, Hyoe and Richie, Donald. eds. <u>A Hundred More
          Things Japanese</u>. Tokyo: Japan Culture Institute, c. 1980.
          215 p. (10 up)

These books do a good job explaining things Japanese
accurately and concisely in two pages which also include an
illustration. The order of entries, however, is arbitrary
and the index is alphabetical by Japanese romanization of
the entry word. There is no English index.

7-009.   Kaula, Edna Mason. <u>Japan Old and New</u>. Cleveland: World, c.
          1970. 157 p. (6 up)

An accurate comparison of traditional and modern Japanese
culture. Since the author's particular interest is art, the
section on art is detailed and quite good. A map and an
index are included.

7-010.   Kirk, Ruth. <u>Japan: Crossroads of East and West</u>. Photographs
          by Bob and Ira Spring. Camden, NJ: Nelson, 1966. 223 p. (4
          up)

I have a strong suspicion that the author does not know
Japanese culture very well. Some of the materials are
collected from such sources as 20th Century Fox movies, and
the author did not check historical evidence. Often
explanations and photographs do not match, and occasionally
explanations are wrong. Should be used with extreme caution.

7-011.   Maki, John M. <u>We the Japanese: Voices from Japan</u>. Voices
          from the Nations. New York: Praeger, 1972. 221 p. (9-12)

See DAILY LIFE, 7-113.

7-012.   Miller, Richard J. and Katoh, Lynn. <u>Japan</u>. New York: Watts,
          c. 1969. 90 p. (4-8)

          This book gives concise information about present-day Japan:
          land, climate, population, historical background, family
          life, sports, education, industries, handicrafts, language,
          literature, arts, and Japan's world role--everything about
          Japan. A certain amount of information included is becoming
          outdated, but because of the broad coverage of topics and
          accuracy of the entries, this small book will be still
          useful. Illustrated with many black-and-white photographs,
          many of them unique to this book. Maps and an index are
          included.

7-013.   Richie, Donald. <u>Introducing Japan</u>. Foreword by Edwin O.
          Reischauer. Text by Donald Richie. New York: Kodansha
          International, c. 1978. 72 p. (6 up)

          The greater part of the book is a pictorial survey of the
          major cities and regions of Japan. The section on each city
          or region is preceded by an introductory paragraph. The
          photographs are extensively annotated. The last part of the
          book consists of one-page essays, with illustrations, on a
          variety of topics including the Japanese house, cuisine,
          sports, government, history, and language. The text is
          concise but very good. All illustrations are in color and
          are of excellent quality.

7-014.   Tuttle, Charles E. <u>Incredible Japan</u>. Tut Books: T. Rev. ed.
          Rutland, VT: Tuttle, 1975. 119 p. (7 up)

          The book is a wide-ranging, informative, and humorous
          introduction to everyday life in Japan. Each topic is
          presented in a one-page explanation and is accompanied by a
          cartoon on the opposite page. Various aspects of food,
          clothing, customs, houses, legends, and amusements are
          discussed. Originally published under the title <u>Japan
          Unbuttoned</u> in 1954.

HISTORY

7-015.   American Heritage, the Editors of, and Reynolds, Robert L.
          <u>Commodore Perry in Japan</u>. New York: American Heritage, c.
          1963. 153 p. (5 up)

This is an account of the first major overseas journey of
the American naval fleet. The "Black Ships" under the
command of Commodore Perry were sent to Japan to force Japan
to end its centuries-old, self-imposed seclusion. The event
is looked at from an American perspective. Many
illustrations of the period: paintings, prints, photographs,
drawings, and maps are included.

7-016.   Bayrd, Edwin and the Editors of the Newsweek Book Division.
          Kyoto. Wonders of Man. New York: Newsweek, c. 1974. 172 p.
          (9 up)

This is a history of Kyoto, and because Kyoto was the
capital of Japan for over 1000 years, it is also a history
of Japan. The book is abundantly illustrated with
photographs of historical buildings, shrines, sculpture, and
artifacts, and reproductions of paintings. The text is
followed by descriptions of Kyoto taken from literature of
various periods, most of which are by Westerners. The
reference section includes a chronology, a guide to Kyoto, a
short bibliography, and an index.

7-017.   Beasley, W.G. The Modern History of Japan. 3rd ed. New York:
          1981. ix, 358 p. (10 up)

A detailed history of nineteenth- and twentieth-century
Japan. Especially strong on foreign relations. The text is
easy to follow so that the lack of illustrative material
other than a few maps is not so noticeable. For advanced
students.

7-018.   Costello, John. The Pacific War. New York: Rawson, Wade
          Publishers, c. 1981. Also available in paperback from
          Morrow (1982). (10 up)

As stated in the preface, "The objective of this book is to
span in a single narrative the century and a half of history
that brought the United States, Great Britain, and other
allied powers to the fatal collision with Japan on Dec. 7,
1941..." and to trace the origins of the war in the
eighteenth century. The book is based on material on the
Pacific War recently made available to scholars for the
first time. The documents show that contrary to common
belief, Roosevelt and his cabinet made a commitment to enter
the war in November, 1941, before the Japanese attack on
Pearl Harbor. Illustrated with black-and-white photographs
and maps. Appended with notes, an extensive bibliography,
and an index.

7-019.   Dilts, Marion May. The Pageant of Japanese History.
         Illustrated with photogravures of Japanese art and
         drawings by Toyojiro Onishi. New York: McKay, 1961. 368 p.
         (6 up)

         This is a detailed work of Japanese history. Although the
         original date of publication is rather old, it is still
         useful because of the accurate and detailed historical facts
         and episodes which are not readily available elsewhere. The
         scarcity of illustrations is regrettable. It includes an
         index, a glossary, a chronological table, and notes.

7-020.   ----------------. Two Japans. Illustrated with photographs.
         New York: McKay, 1963. vii, 246 p. (10-12)

         This book covers two periods in the modern history of Japan:
         Japan's emergence from isolation (ca. 1850-1873); and Japan
         in the world community (ca. 1950-1963). The book is based on
         original documents and is very accurate and highly
         informative. Readable and interesting. Extensive footnotes
         and an index are included. Illustrated with old drawings, a
         map, and recent photographs.

7-021.   Earhart, H. Byron. Japanese Religion: Unity and Diversity.
         The Religious Life of Man Series. Third ed. Belmont, CA:
         Wadsworth Publishing, c. 1982. xii, 272 p. (10 up)

         A general introduction to the history and dynamics of
         Japanese religion written in laymen's language. The various
         native and imported traditions which have interacted to form
         a distinctive Japanese religious heritage are explored. The
         chapter on persistent themes in Japanese religious history
         might be of particular interest to many readers. Appended
         with an extensive annotated bibliography on Japanese
         religion, study questions, and an extensive index. An
         excellent book.

7-022.   Gibson, Michael. The Rise of Japan. New York: Putnam, c.
         1972. 128 p. (6 up)

         This is a history of Japan from the time of Commodore
         Perry's expedition to Japan (1853) to the end of the
         Occupation of Japan by the Allied Forces in 1952. A short
         introduction summarizes the history of Japan prior to 1853.
         The book covers the cultural, economic, and political
         aspects of the period as well as the social life and
         customs. Well illustrated with black-and-white photographs
         and reproductions of drawings. Includes maps, a table of
         events, short biographies of major personnel, a glossary, a
         bibliography and an index. The addition of headings on one
         side of each page makes it easy to skim.

7-023.   Goldston, Robert. Pearl Harbor! A World Focus Book. New
            York: Watts, c. 1972. 90 p. (7-12)

            A brief, but accurate history of Japan from ancient times to
            the end of World War II, with emphasis on the events that
            led to the attack on Pearl Harbor in 1941. The author is
            very knowledgeable about the history of Japan and has a wide
            and detailed knowledge of and good insight into world
            history as well. Includes many informative illustrations,
            both drawings and photographs. Appended with a chronological
            table covering Japanese history from 660 B.C. to 1945. Also
            includes a list of suggested readings and a detailed index.

7-024.   Guillan, Robert. I Saw Tokyo Burning: An Eyewitness
            Narrative from Pearl Harbor to Hiroshima. Translated by
            William Bylon. New York: Doubleday, 1981. xii, 298 p. (10
            up)

            This is an invaluable first-hand account of Japan during the
            Second World War by a French correspondent forced to remain
            in Tokyo for the duration of the war by the outbreak of
            hostilities. He describes the shock felt by the Japanese at
            the proclamation of war against the United States, the
            subsequent enthusiasm following victories in Hong Kong and
            the Phillipines. He also includes the rumors and gossip of
            the time. The last section of the book shows how the
            Japanese survived, rebuilt their nation from the ruins, and
            even "Americanized" in a short time.

7-025.   Hall, John Whitney. Japan: From Prehistory to Modern Times.
            Delacorte World History. A Delta Book. New York: Dell
            Publishing, c. 1970. xii, 397 p. (10 up)

            An excellent general history of Japan, informative and
            well-written. Appended with a chronology, a glossary, an
            extensive bibliography, and an index. Perhaps it is too
            detailed for use as a high-school text, but would be an
            excellent first source for further information for both
            student and teacher. Highly recommended.

7-026.   Haven, Thomas R.H. Valley of Darkness: The Japanese People
            and World War Two. New York: Norton, c. 1978. xi, 280 p.
            (10 up)

            An extremely well-researched, accurate, and well-written
            account of wartime life in Japan. Beginning with the Sino-
            Japanese conflict in 1937, the author objectively follows
            the lives of some Japanese citizens during World War II. He
            chronicles the effects of the minute rules and regulations
            instituted by the government to support the war effort. The

last chapter is an assessment of the changes wrought by this
futile war. This book is powerful, the topics well-selected,
and the arrangement well-thought out. Highly recommended.

7-027.   Hempel, Rose. The Golden Age of Japan 794-1192. Translated
          by Katherine Watson. New York: Rizzoli, c. 1983. 251 p.
          (10 up)

          See ART, 1-010.

7-028.   Icenhower, Joseph B. Perry and the Open Door to Japan. A
          World Focus Book. New York: Watts, c. 1973. 64 p. (6-12)

          The details of the earliest encounter of Japan and the
          United States, Perry's arrival in Tokyo Bay, and the signing
          of the Treaty of Kanagawa. Includes a bibliography and
          index. Well illustrated with photographs and drawings.
          Appended with a map of Japan and the text of the Treaty of
          Kanagawa. Good.

7-029.   Kidder, Edward. Ancient Japan. The Making of the Past.
          Oxford: Elsevier, Phaidon, 1977. 152 p. (7-12)

          The author is a professor of archaeology who lived in Japan
          for many years. His book presents the history of ancient
          Japan from the Palaeolithic period (ca. 500 B.C.) to the
          Heian period (twelfth century A.D.) as derived from
          archeological data. Life, culture, mythology, religion, and
          history are discussed. Abundant illustrations (203 total,
          134 in color) enhance this authoritative work. Includes a
          good glossary, a list for further reading, a chronological
          table, and an index.

7-030.   Leonard, Jonathan Norton and the Editors of Time-Life Books.
          Early Japan. Revised ed. New York: Time-Life Books, 1976.
          191 p. (6 up)

          This is a highly detailed and accurate history of Japan from
          earliest times to 1603. An exquisitely illustrated book with
          many color illustrations, each accompanied by an informative
          explanation. Includes a bibliography, chronological table,
          and general index. Highly recommended.

7-031.   Lum, Peter. Six Centuries in East Asia: China, Japan and
          Korea from the 14 Century to 1912. New York: Phillips, c.
          1973. 256 p. (9 up)

          The history of East Asia (China, Japan, and Korea) from the
          fourteenth century to 1912 is well described in this concise
          book. Facts and events are often explained in the context of
          East Asia or world politics. The text is very easy to read
          and understand. Illustrated with black-and-white

reproductions of paintings and photographs. Appended with a
chronological table, a glossary, a bibliography and an
index. Highly recommended.

7-032.   Meyer, Milton W. Japan: A Concise History. A Littlefield,
          Adams Quality Paperback; no. 318. Revised ed. Totowa, NJ:
          Littlefield, Adams, 1976. xi, 265 p. (10 up)

The original edition of this book was published in 1966.
This revised edition changed the organization of the book
and subdivided each of the four parts (traditional, feudal,
modern, and postwar Japan) into three to six chapters. There
is a short introductory chapter for readers who are not
familiar with Japan. The book provides a good introduction
to the history of Japan. There is a good and extensive
glossary at the end of each chapter. It is appended with
charts and tables, however, there are no illustrations which
make this otherwise good book less attractive. A
bibliography and an index.

7-033.   Minear, Richard H. Victor's Justice: The Tokyo War Crimes
          Trial. Princeton, NJ: Princeton University Press, c. 1971.
          xv, 229 p. (10 up)

This is the first serious study of the Tokyo War Crimes
Trials. After extensive and careful research of the trial
documents, Minear concludes that the Japanese were not tried
for atrocities, but for war itself; not for unjustifiable
wartime acts, but for aggression. A provocative book which
questions the feasibility of war-crime trials.

7-034.   Murakami, Hyoe. Japan: The Years of Trial 1919-52. New York:
          Kodansha International, c. 1982. 246 p. (10 up)

This is a detailed political history of Japan during most of
the twentieth century. The author clearly shows how Japan
walked step-by-step on the road to war and tries to explain
why Japan followed the path it did. Japan's behavior is
explained in large part by its late arrival on the
international scene. The subsequent defeat of Japan at the
end of World War II is cited as a contributing factor to the
swift independence of Southeast Asian and Pacific countries.
Includes a chronology and detailed index. The bibliography
lists primarily Japanese readings.

7-035.   Murakami, Hyoe and Harper, Thomas J. eds. Great historical
          Figures of Japan. Tokyo: The Japan Culture Institute, c.
          1978. xii, 327 p. (10 up)

Lives of forty-one prominent figures in the long history of
Japan are discussed. Included are emperors, shoguns,
aristocrats, ladies-in-waiting, officials, bureaucrats,

warriors, scholars, religious leaders, poets, novelists, tea
masters, riot organizers, and business leaders. The
biographies are presented in chronological order. Each of
the biographical sketches is written by an authority in the
field who discusses the historical setting of his subject's
life. This is a useful book and a welcome addition to the
small collection of biographies of Japanese available in
English.

7-036.   Nakamoto, Hiroko. My Japan: 1930-1951. As told to Mildred
          Mastin Pace. New York: McGraw-Little, c. 1970. 157 p. (5
          up)

          See HIROSHIMA, 7-064.

7-037.   Newman, Robert. The Japanese: People of the Three Treasures.
          Drawings by Mamoru Funai. New York: Atheneum, c. 1964. 187
          p. (6 up)

          A detailed history of Japan from the mythical period to the
          end of the Edo period, 1867, with a unique approach.
          Includes detailed accounts of historical and mythical tales.
          The text is good and accurate except for some
          mispronunciations of names and words. The author shows
          particular interest in the Three Treasures which are the
          symbols of the Japanese emperor's divinity and power.
          Information on bushido (the knightly code) and Shintoism is
          particularly detailed and well-written for young people.
          Appended are notes on Japanese names and pronunciation, a
          list of major periods of Japanese history, and a list of
          further reading; includes a map and an index. Recommended.

7-038.   Nish, Ian. The Story of Japan. The Story of...London: Faber
          and Faber, c. 1968. 238 p. (10 up)

          A well-researched history of Japan from its beginnings to
          1968. Chapters are subdivided into sections which makes the
          book easy to read. There are few illustrations, mainly
          black-and-white photographs, and three small maps. Includes
          a detailed reading list and an index.

7-039.   The Pacific War Research Society. Comp. Japan's Longest Day.
          Palo Alto, CA: Kodansha International, c. 1968. 339 p. (9
          up)

          Originally published in Japanese as Nihon no Ichiban Nagai
          Hi in 1965. This is a dramatic, detailed record of the
          twenty-four hours that preceded the Emperor's broadcast, on
          August 15, 1945, in which he announced that Japan had
          surrendered to the Allies on the previous day. For
          interested readers.

7-040.   Perry, John Curtis. <u>Beneath the Eagle's Wings: Americans in</u>
<u>Occupied Japan</u>. Illustrated with photographs. New York:
Dodd, Mead, c. 1980. xvi, 253 p. (10 up)

This is a sensitive analysis of the extraordinarily
successful Allied Occupation of Japan from August 1945 to
the spring of 1952 during which the Allies tried to change
Japan in some rather basic ways. The author studied a
tremendous number of documents and has analyzed the meaning
of the American Occupation of Japan for both Americans and
Japanese. The book includes detailed notes, a bibliography
for further research, and an index. Illustrated with many
black-and-white photographs which cannot be found in other
books.

7-041.   Powell, Brian. <u>Modern Japan: A Brief History from A.D. 800</u>
<u>to the Present Day</u>. The Young Historian Books. Drawings by
Elizabeth Hammond. New York: Day, 1969. 112 p. (6-12)

The book starts where J.E. Kidder's <u>Ancient Japan</u>, also
published by John Day, left off. The book, however, is
incorrectly titled; the nineteenth century, and not the
ninth century, is generally considered to be the beginning
of modern Japan. The book also contains little information
after 1945. Illustrations are mainly drawings with some
photographs and wood-block prints.

7-042.   Reischauer. Edwin O. <u>Japan: The History of the Nation</u>. 3rd
ed. New York: Knopf, c. 1981. xiii, 428 p. (10 up)

This book was written by an established historian of Japan
who was also the U.S. ambassador to Japan from 1961 to 1966.
The book is arranged in three sections: Traditional Japan,
Modernizing Japan, and Postwar Japan. Readable and
interesting. Includes maps and many drawings and
photographs. It is appended with an extensive chronology, a
good bibliography and a detailed index.

7-043.   ---------------. <u>The Japanese</u>. Cambridge, MA: The Berknap
Press of Harvard University Press, 1977. 443 p. (10 up)

This is an earlier work of this famous scholar and former
ambassador to Japan. The book focuses on what the Japanese
are like today and how Japan fits into the contemporary
world. The book is divided into five major sections, each of
which is subdivided by topic into short chapters. The first
two sections provide information on the physical aspects of
Japan and the historical background. The three remaining
sections, the bulk of the book, is about society and
politics in modern Japan and Japan's current involvement in
the international community. A suggested reading list is
selective and current. Informative and accurate.

7-044.   Roberts, John G. Black Ships and Rising Sun: The Opening of
          Japan to the West. New York: Julian Messner, c. 1971. 191
          p. (6-12)

          The forced end to Japan's policy of seclusion by the U.S.
          naval squadron in 1853 was the beginning of Japan's
          transformation into one of the world's great industrial
          powers. The initial confrontation between Japan and the West
          exposed Japan's weakness vis-a-vis the West. Japan had to
          Westernize quickly to ensure that Western powers treated her
          as an equal. This book tells the story of this period in
          Japanese history and explains how Japan was able to avoid
          becoming a colony of Western powers. The author's style is
          easy to read. Includes plates, portraits, and drawings of
          some of the historical events of the period.

7-045.   Sansom, G.B. Japan: A Short Cultural History. Stanford, CA:
          Stanford University Press, 1978. xv, 548 p. (12 up)

          A book by one of the most qualified authors on the subject
          of Japanese cultural history. The book was first published
          in 1931 and the last major revision was done in 1952. While
          the emphasis in this work is on cultural aspects of Japanese
          history, the extensive general historical information
          provided makes this work a more complete general
          introduction to Japanese history than the title would
          suggest. Some illustrations and an index. For advanced
          students.

7-046.   Schirokauer, Conrad. A Brief History of Chinese and Japanese
          Civilizations. New York: Harcourt Brace Jovanovich, c.
          1978. xxi, 662 p. (10 up)

          An introductory text on the civilizations of China and Japan
          which covers the broad spectrum of human activity.
          Information is provided on art and thought as well as
          economic, political, and social history. Each chapter is
          devoted to one of the countries during one historical time
          period and runs, on average, 25 pages long. The text is very
          readable and the many maps and illustrations complement the
          text nicely. Each chapter is preceded by a time line. An
          excellent, extensive annotated suggested reading list is
          provided as is a comprehensive index.

7-047.   Tamarin, Alfred. Japan and the United States: Early
          Encounters 1791-1860. New York: Macmillan, c. 1970. vii,
          260 p. (6 up)

Extensive account of the early relationship between Japan
and the United States. It is well researched and documented.
Illustrated with many colored woodblock prints, old
drawings, and photographs. A list of further readings,
sources and notes, and an index are included.

7-048.   Tames, Richard. Japan: In the Twentieth Century. Twentieth
          Century World History. London: Batsford Academic and
          Educational, c. 1981. 96 p. (7-12)

          This is an extremely accurate, well-balanced insightful book
          on twentieth century Japan for junior and senior high school
          students. Each chapter is well thought-out and is
          accompanied by several excellent questions. The book is
          well-illustrated with maps, black-and-white photographs,
          drawings, and tables of figures. It is appended with a
          chronological table, bibliography, and an index. Most highly
          recommended.

7-049.   ----------------. Japan Today. London: Kaye & Ward in
          association with Hicks Smith & Sons (Australia and New
          Zealand), c. 1976. 95 p. (5-9)

          A general introduction to Japan. Introduces the land and the
          people of Japan, provides a history of the country, and
          discusses the problems Japan faces as a highly
          industrialized country. Extremely informative and accurate,
          and written in readable English. Richly illustrated with
          black-and-white photographs, each accompanied by a concise
          explanation. Includes maps and diagrams. Appended with a
          chronological table and short list of further readings.

7-050.   Tomlin, E, W.F. Japan. Nations and People. New York: Walker,
          1973. 176 p. (10 up)

          This book deals with Japan from its prehistoric days to the
          present. An extremely accurate, well-researched, and well-
          balanced book. Written by a man who lived in Japan for years
          and has an extensive knowledge of the country. Includes good
          footnotes, a detailed glossary of Japanese words, a who's
          who, and an extensive index.

7-051.   Totman, Conrad. Japan Before Perry: A Short History.
          Berkeley: University of California Press, c. 1981. xv, 246
          p. (10 up)

          The author "examines the complex process by which the
          scattered and small groups of illiterate people who occupied
          the islands of Japan...developed into the densely populated,
          elaborately organized, and highly sophisticated society of
          early nineteenth-century Japan." The book focuses on growth
          and fundamental change in premodern Japanese society,

relating the history in broad strokes rather than in
details. The summary of Japanese history is well done. The
meaning and importance of Japan's early history for the
better understanding of contemporary Japan is well
displayed. Footnotes, a glossary, and an index.

7-052.   ----------------. Tokugawa Ieyasu. South San Francisco: Heian
          International, 1983. xvi, 205 p. (10 up)

This is a biography of the founder of the last and most
successful samurai government in Japanese history, the
Tokugawa Shogunate (1600 to 1868). The author, who is one of
the most important historians of the Tokugawa period, has
provided a broad history of the period of the founding of
the shogunate while focusing on Ieyasu. The century
preceding the establishment of the Tokugawa shogunate was a
time of disunity in Japan, a time when military men fought,
sometimes daily, to consolidate and expand their control
over land and men, all in the hope that ultimately they
would control the country. This book explores how and why
Ieyasu succeeded while those before him failed. Clavell's
novel Shogun is set in this time and Totman relates Ieyasu's
meeting with Will Adams, "Anjin-san" of the novel.

7-053.   Varley, Paul H. Japanese Culture. Third ed. Honolulu:
          University of Hawaii Press, c. 1984. 331 p. (12 up)

Japanese Culture is a survey, for the general reader, of the
history of cultural life in Japan from the emergence of
Japanese civilization to the present. It traces the cultural
development through the ages in the areas of religion,
thought, literature, theatre, cinema, the visual arts, and
the other forms of culture and art. The author relates
cultural developments to political and institutional trends.
The new edition gives the most balanced and comprehensive
presentation of the history of Japanese culture available in
English. Notes follow the text. Includes a glossary, a
bibliography, and a detailed index. For advanced students.

7-054.   ----------------. The Onin War: History of its Origins and
          Background with a Selective Translation of the Chronicle
          of Onin. Studies in Oriental Culture. New York: Columbia
          University Press, 1967. x, 238 p. (10 up)

A well-researched book on the war (1467-1477) which weakened
the central government almost to the point of extinction and
which marks the beginning of the century-long period of
anarchy known as Sengoku ("the country at war"). The
translation of the Chronicle of Onin is readable and
interesting, providing a clear picture of the suffering and

chaos of the times. Appended with a glossary, bibliography, notes, and an index. An epilogue provides brief information on the postwar years. Highly recommended.

7-055.   Washow, Steven and David C. Bromwell, with A.J. Tudisco. Japan Emerges: A Concise History of Japan from its Origin to the Present. The Asia Emerges Series: 3. Berkeley: Diablo Press, c. 1974. 1979 printing. xiii, 183 p. (9 up)

This text was first published in 1964 as part of Asia Emerges. It was revised and expanded in 1974. It covers all Japanese history and includes the cultural as well as political, social, and economic aspects of the history. Each chapter covers one historical period. Illustrated with black-and-white photographs, reproductions of drawing and paintings, and maps of Japan and Asia. Appended with various source materials, tables, a glossary, a bibliography, and an index. Very readable text.

7-056.   Wheeler, Keith and the Editors of Time-Life Books. The Fall of Japan. World War II, Time-Life Books. Alexandria, VA: Time-Life Books, c. 1983. 207 p. (7-12)

This book relates the events leading to the surrender of Japan at the end of World War II from the perspective of both the Japanese and the Americans. In the spring of 1945, Japan was a nation on the edge of starvation, and the continued deterioration in living conditions was a major factor shaping Japanese war strategy. In the United States, the decisions on war strategy revolved around the question of whether or not to use the newly developed atomic bomb. Conditions in Japan after the surrender are also described. Illustrated with black-and-white photographs and colored drawings by survivors and witnesses of the atomic bombings of Hiroshima and Nagasaki. Includes a bibliography and an index.

7-057.   ----------------. The Road to Tokyo. World War II, Time-Life Books. Alexandria, VA: Time-Life Books, c. 1979. 208 p. (7 up)

This is a careful and fair account of the campaigns on Iwo Jima and Okinawa during World War II. The author was a war correspondent who was critically wounded at Iwo Jima. His writing is objective and readable. Numerous good maps and excellent and powerful photographs from various sources are included. The photographs are sometimes as eloquent as the text which accompanies them. Appended with an extensive bibliography and an index.

7-058.   Wiencek, Henry. The Lords of Japan. Treasures of the World. Chicago: Stonehenge Press, c. 1982. 176 p. (10 up)

This book treats the lives of the ruling class of Japan from early history to the early seventeenth century. Various aspects of their lives are considered: pastimes, art and architecture, gardens, armor, etc. The book is extravagantly illustrated. Appended with a chronology and an index.

7-059.   Williams, Barry. Emerging Japan. Modern Times. New York: McGraw-Hill, c. 1968. 143 p. (6-12)

Covers Japan from the opening of the country in 1853 to the birth of the new Japan after World War II. The arrangement of the book is good; the chapters are short and are subdivided with appropriate headings. Includes various miscellaneous but interesting material not normally found in similar works of this size. An index and a short bibliography are included.

HIROSHIMA

7-060.   Buckner, Karl. The Day of the Bomb. Translated by Frances Lobb. Princeton, NJ: Van Nostrand, c. 1961. English ed. 1962. 89 p. (7 up)

Translated from Sadako will Leben. This is the story of a family which lived in Hiroshima when the atomic bomb was dropped. The story is told in flashback which makes the book difficult to read. The last half of the book concentrates on the young girl of the family who is dying of radiation disease. The monstrous destructive power and inhumanity of nuclear weapons are made clear.

7-061.   Japan Broadcasting Corporation. Unforgettable Fire: Pictures Drawn by Atomic Bomb Survivors. New York: Pantheon, c. 1977. 1981 printing. 110 p. (All ages)

Translation of Goka O Mita. The book is the outcome of an exhibit sponsored by the Japan Broadcasting Corporation in 1974. It is a collection of 104 pictures drawn by people who were in Hiroshima when the atomic bomb was dropped. The pictures are preceded by a short article, "Hiroshima on That Day", which provides a good introduction. The pictures and notes eloquently convey the message of "No more Hiroshimas." An extremely powerful, unforgettable book. Highly recommended.

7-062.   Lifton, Betty Jean. Return to Hiroshima. Photographs by
          Eikoh Hosoe. New York: Atheneum, c. 1970. 91 p. (5 up)

          Mrs. Lifton, with the cooperation of the famous Japanese
          photographer, Eikoh Hosoe, has produced a quiet but powerful
          message about Hiroshima, the atomic bomb, its victims, and
          its survivors. Through interview and excellent photographs,
          the author shows how things were at the time the bomb was
          dropped and how things were twenty years later. After
          reading this book, the reader is left to ponder nuclear war.

7-063.   Maruki, Toshi. Hiroshima no Pika. Words and pictures by
          Toshi Maruki. New York: Lothrop, Lee & Shepard Books, c.
          1980. Unpaged. (K-6)

          Mrs. Maruki, the artist/author, has been very active in
          campaigning for nuclear disarmament and world peace using
          her paintings as the medium. "It (Hiroshima) can't happen
          again if no one drops the bomb." Both illustrations and text
          are excellent; it tells the story of a young girl and her
          family and their experiences in Hiroshima during the first
          few days after the atomic bomb was dropped.

6-064.   Nakamoto, Hiroko. My Japan: 1930-1951. As told to Mildred
          Mastin Pace. New York: McGraw-Little, c. 1970. 157 p. (5
          up)

          The personal experiences of a Japanese woman who survived
          the atomic bomb in Hiroshima. The author records her life
          and that of others from 1930 through 1951. This book will
          help American students understand what happened to the
          Japanese people during this period.

7-065.   Osada, Arata. Children of Hiroshima. Harper Colophon Books.
          New York: Harper Row, 1982. xxxv, 333 p. (4 up)

          This book was originally published in Japanese in 1951. It
          is a compilation of accounts written by Japanese children
          and young adults who survived the atomic attack on
          Hiroshima. It was compiled by Osada in the hope of banning
          nuclear arms and securing world peace. He chose the work of
          children "whose thought had not yet been tainted with any
          specific political ideology or view of the world" to present
          his message. The accounts are grouped by school level, from
          primary through college. Should be read by everyone.

7-066.   Stein, Conrad R. Hiroshima. World at War. Chicago: Childrens
          Press, c. 1982. 48 p. (3-6)

          The author traces the history of the atomic bomb, the
          decision to drop it, and the aftereffects. The book is
          written in an easy style that even small children can

understand. The author's quiet but powerful anti-war message comes through clearly. Words of President Truman, quoted in the book, should be carefully considered. "It (the atomic bomb) was just the same as getting a bigger gun than the other fellow...and that's what it was used for. Nothing else but an artillery weapon." Many photographs and an index.

TEXTBOOKS

7-067.   Ashby, Gwynneth M. Looking at Japan. Looking at Other
         Countries. Philadelphia: Lippincott, 1969. 62 p. (4-6)

         This book is accurate, informative, and easy to read because
         it is written in simple sentences. Illustrations are
         selected with a fresh perspective, and the author's
         openmindedness shows through. Some facts and figures, now
         outdated, are printed on the end papers but the text itself
         includes few statistics, and for this reason remains usable.
         Good photographs and a good map are included.

7-068.   Brown, Delmer M. Japan. Today's World in Focus, Japan.
         Boston; Ginn, c. 1968. vi, 122 p. (4 up)

         This is an excellent summary covering all aspects of Japan
         and is accurate, informative, and well-written. Still one of
         the best of this type of books, but because of its age, the
         section in chapter nine on the economy and some statistical
         data is no longer usable. It is appended with a glossary of
         Japanese words, a chronological table of key events in
         Japanese history, and a bibliography. Highly recommended.

7-069.   Buell, Hal. Young Japan. New York: Dodd & Mead, c. 1961. 64
         p. (3-6)

         Accurate, infromative and readable book which is still
         usable despite its age. The author was a photo editor in
         Asia for the Associated Press and his pictures capture what
         it is like to grow up in Japan with its mixture of
         traditional and modern ways. A good introduction to Japanese
         culture.

7-070.   Davidson, Judith. Japan: Where East Meets West. Discovering
         Our Heritage Series. Minneapolis: Dillon Press, 1983. 139
         p. (3-6)

This is an up-to-date introduction to Japanese culture and history for young people. It has many useful features such as a table of facts about Japan, a map, a table of Japanese syllabary, addresses of Japanese consulates in the United States and Canada, and a glossary. It includes black-and-white photographs, a bibliography, and a detailed index. There are some mistakes which should be noted: pages 13 and 50 have Japanese sentences, both of which are ungrammatical; pages 43-44 incorrectly lists the social divisions of feudal society. It should read "warriors (and priests), farmers, artisans and merchants"; page 61 on the children's festival Shichi-go-san should read five-year old boys and seven-year-old girls. The discussion of page 18 on pets indicates that Japanese children adopt large, horned cockroaches as pets. Most likely the insect adopted is a beetle since the Japanese do not like cockroaches.

7-071. Edelman, Lily. Japan in Story and Pictures. Foreword by Roma Gans. Illustrated with photographs. New York: Harcourt, Brace, c. 1953. vi, 56 p. (3-6)

Excellent text despite its age. The statistics as well as the information on industry and housing is outdated but the rest of the text remains useful. Used with a more recent social studies book, this text can provide the basis of a study of the changes Japan experienced in the last thirty years. All the Japanese words are spelled correctly. The only two words which should not have been used are: Mama-san and papa-san, meaning mother and father.

7-072. Friskey, Margaret. Welcome to Japan. Welcome to the World Books. Sketches by Lois Axeman. Chicago: Childrens Press, c. 1975. 48 p. (2-5)

A very short text is laid out opposite full-page color photographs. A map. Not very informative.

7-073. Greenblatt, Miriam. Japan. People of the World. Scott Foresman Spectra Program. Glenview, IL: Scott, Foresman, c. 1975. 143 p. (4-9)

The text deals only with contemporary Japan and covers many aspects of modern life. Many accounts of lives of real people are included as well as excerpts from various books and articles. Each chapter begins with a guide to the reading, and questions are included for each topic within the chapter and for summing up the chapter as well. Although there are minor mistakes and the text is getting a little old, the book still offers useful information. Illustrated with maps and many photographs and drawings.

7-074.   Greene, Carol. <u>Japan</u>. Enchantment of the World. Chicago:
          Childrens Press, c. 1983. 127 p. (5-9)

          By far one of the best of this type of book. It is up-to-
          date and includes a broad range of information on the
          geography, history, economy, and culture of modern Japan.
          The text is interesting and written clearly in short
          sentences. Illustrations are excellent, recent, color
          photographs. Includes detailed maps, a map key, a "Mini-
          facts at a glance" (which is an excellent summary of the
          book), and an index. The only small mistake is in the
          summary which says, "Meals are eaten <u>off trays</u>." This is not
          done anymore except for special occasions or at Japanese
          inns.

7-075.   Hoare, Sophy. <u>Japan: The Land and Its People</u>. London:
          Macdonald Educational. Published in the United States by
          Silver Burdett, Morristown, NJ: c. 1975. 61 p. (5 up)

          This is by far one of the best books of its size for use by
          a wide range of readers. Many topics are considered and each
          topic is treated in two concise, accurate pages of text.
          Includes many statistics, and most are still useful.
          Abundantly illustrated with good photographs and
          reproductions of paintings, all of which are accompanied by
          good explanations. Unfortunately many of the drawings in the
          book contain stereotypical mistakes. An index. Despite its
          faults still highly recommended.

7-076.   Jacobsen, Karen. <u>Japan</u>. A New True Book. Chicago: Childrens
          Press, c. 1982. 45 p. (1-6)

          A well-organized book that has a short, clear, text that
          could easily be read by second graders. It includes
          information on the geography, history, culture, and
          industries of Japan and is illustrated with many good
          photographs. It includes a map and a detailed list of
          important Japanese and English words. Well-indexed. Highly
          recommended.

7-077.   Jakeman, Alan. <u>Getting to Know Japan</u>. Revised ed.
          Illustrated by Don Lambo. New York: Coward, McCann, c.
          1971. 64 p. (5-7)

          The original edition of this social studies textbook was
          full of errors and very little of the book was revised and
          changed in this newer 1971 edition. Both the text and the
          illustrations are hopelessly inaccurate. Appended with a
          short glossary, pronunciation table, short chronological
          table and an index. Do not use.

7-078.   Kublin, Hyman. Japan: Selected Readings. World Regional
         Studies. Revised ed. Boston: Houghton Mifflin, c. 1973.
         xi, 244 p. (9-12)

         Intended to be used as a companion volume to a regional
         study text. Primary and secondary source material is
         provided to allow high school students "to explore the
         origins, way of life, and the aspirations as well as the
         achievements of the Japanese." Each section is introduced by
         a short essay which provides a context for the subsequent
         selections. About half the material is on the period after
         1853. Good questions for study and discussion are included
         at the end of the book. Index.

7-079.   Master, Robert V. Japan in Pictures. Visual Geography
         Series. Revised ed. New York: Sterling, 1978. 64 p. (5-9)

         Although this book supposedly has been revised eight times
         since 1961, it has gone through very little change. Most of
         the text and many of the photographs are the same as those
         in earlier editions. The total number of pages has also
         remained the same. The book is primarily pictorial (black-
         and-white illustrations), but there is accurate and usable
         information in the very general text. Covers the history of
         Japan, the country, people, art and literature, the economy,
         and government.

7-080.   Mears, Helen. The First Book of Japan. Pictures by kathleen
         Elgin. New York: Watts, 1953. 68 p. (3-6)

         Both the text and illustrations include numerous silly
         mistakes. Drawings, and not photographs, are used as
         illustrations and they are better representations of late
         nineteenth-century Japan than of modern Japan.

7-081.   Minear, Richard. Through Japanese Eyes. Leon E. Clard,
         General editor. New York: Praeger Publishers, c. 1974. 2
         v. bound in one. (6 up)

         A well-selected compilation of articles, most previously
         published elsewhere, which provides the reader with the
         opportunity to view Japan's modern history from the Japanese
         perspective. The material is divided into two volumes.
         Volume 1, The Past: The Road from Isolation, covers the
         nineteenth- and twentieth-centuries to the 1960s. Volume 2,
         The Present: Coping With Affluence, deals primarily with
         economic conditions of the 1970s. Highly recommended.

7-082.   Peterson, Lorraine D. How People Live in Japan. Basic
         Concepts Series Westchester, IL: Benefic Press, c. 1972.
         93 p. (3-9)

Although this book was published in 1972, some of the
information is from the early 1950s and outdated. Some of
the statements are oversimplified and sometimes include a
narrow American view of international relations as in the
following: "One way to help the people (of Japan) decide
(which side to be with) is to educate them to see what
Communism does" (p. 8). "We hope to show Japan that it is
better to have a democracy and freedom rather than
Communism. We hope to help Japan be a barrier to Communism"
(p. 89). Some of the illustrations are inaccurate. Questions
are included at the end of each chapter section as well as a
summary of basic concepts, and an index.

7-083.   Pitts, Forrest R. Japan. Fideler Social Studies. World
         Cultures: Basic Area Studies. Grand Rapids, MI: Fideler,
         c. 1981. 192 p. (5-9)

Very good, well-rounded book on Japan for use in a wide
grade span of social studies classes. The book is divided
into four parts: Land and Climate, History and Government,
People and Their Way of Life, and Earning a Living. The
information is new and quite accurate since this book is
often updated. The book is set up so that children are
encouraged to think for themselves although some of the
questions posed are too obvious. There was only one minute
mistake on page 92, in the explanation of a photograph which
says charcoal stove instead of wood stove.

7-084.   Ryan, Frank L. and Clark, James I. Windows on Japan. Social
         Studies Readers. Boston: Houghton Mifflin, c. 1979. 79 p.
         (2-6)

This book is intended for classroom use. It is written in
simple English and includes much up-to-date information
about Japan and its people. Occasionally, the authors are
too eager to suggest conclusions, and some parts of the text
are a little artificial. A letter which was supposed to be
from a Japanese girl to an American pen pal says, "On
Children's Day, Japanese cut paper in the shape of carp and
put them on the pole." But as the illustration on the
opposite page shows, carp are made of cloth with colorful
streamers also made of cloth and they swim in the air when
there is wind. Accompanied by a teacher's guide.

7-085.   Steinberg, Rafael. Japan. Illustrated with photographs. New
         York: Macmillan, c. 1969. 138 p. (6 up)

This book is an accurate description of Japan that treats
all aspects of Japanese culture and society; it also has a
chapter on the problems Japan faces. Included are a
bibliography of further readings, a general index, and a map
of Japan.

7-086.   Storry, Richard. <u>Japan</u>. Countries of Today. New York: White,
          c. 1969. 128 p. (6-9)

          While the sections on the economy and industry are now
          outdated, the rest of the text is excellent and is still
          usable and highly informative. The author gives a good
          overview of Japan's history and offers deep insight. Many
          black-and-white photographs and an index are included.

7-087.   Vaugham, Josephine Budd. <u>The Land and the People of Japan</u>.
          Portraits of the Nation Series. Revised ed. Philadelphia:
          Lippincott, 1972. 158 p. (5-9)

          For this edition, some chapters have been added and others
          have been reorganized and rewritten, but there is still not
          much difference between the 1952 edition and this one. Most
          of the illustrations are either taken from the former
          edition or are photographs that must have been taken in the
          1950s. Explanation is often detailed, but even in new
          chapters such as that on education, there are mistakes like
          "Children enter elementary school at the age of six, pass
          through eight grades, then go on to their secondary
          education of four years." There has never been such a system
          in Japan. Compulsory education in Japan is six years for
          elementary school, and then three years of secondary school.
          Not much new information has been added, and the figures
          quoted are not current, which makes them less meaningful.

7-088.   Walker, Richard I. <u>Ancient Japan and Its Influence in Modern
          Times</u>. Illustrated with photographs. New York: Watts, c.
          1975. 86 p. (5 up)

          Mostly accurate and detailed observation, but there are
          occasional overstatements. Full of black-and-white
          illustrations. Included are a map, a chronology of ancient
          Japan for 4000 B.C. through 1600 A.D., and an index. A
          useful book, but should be used with caution.

7-089.   Watson, Werner Jane. <u>Japan: Islands of the Rising Sun</u>.
          Champaign, IL: Garrard, c. 1968. 112 p. (3-6)

          This is a detailed, informative, generally accurate, and
          readable book. Although most of the information is still
          accurate and usable, sometimes Japan is drawn in a too
          idealistic way. A map and a general index are included.
          There are a few mistakes in the text. In an essay at the end
          of the book, the author calls Mrs. Iuchi Mama-san Iuchi. The
          English word "Mama" has been included in Japanese, but when
          you add a honorific "san" to this particular word, it means
          a bar hostess.

GEOGRAPHY AND DESCRIPTION

7-090.   Boardman, Gwenn R. Living in Tokyo. Camden, NJ: Nelson, c.
         1970. 198 p. (4-9)

         Although the title is Living in Tokyo, the information
         included in this book is not limited to Tokyo. Daily life is
         placed at the center of this book, and the author succeeded
         in describing it well. The text is fairly good and
         informative. Includes a map of Inner-Tokyo, and an index.
         Illustrated with black-and-white photographs.

7-091.   Gibbon, David. Japan: A Picture Book to Remember Her By. A
         Picture Book to Remember Her By. Produced by Ted Smart.
         New York: Crescent, 1978. Unpaged. (7 up)

         This is a pictorial work with a minimum of text. There is a
         one-page introduction to Japan and each photograph has a
         brief and accurate explanation. The pictures cover a wide
         range of subjects from scenery, buildings, gardens, statues,
         and stores to people but, unfortunately, they are not
         arranged in any order. There are some mistakes in the
         spelling of place and proper names.

7-092.   Hearn, Lafcadio. Glimpses of Unfamiliar Japan. Rutland, VT:
         Tuttle, 1976. 699 p. (10 up)

         Hearn was an American who went to Japan after the country
         was forceably opened in the 1850s, became enamored with the
         culture, and eventually became a naturalized citizen. His
         observations of Japan during the dynamic Meiji period can be
         used as the base from which the extent and the direction of
         the change in Japan during the last century can be judged.

7-093.   Kobayashi, Fusae. Living in Tokyo. Living in Famous Cities.
         East Essex, England: Wayland, c. 1980. 52 p. (2-6)

         Up-to-date, accurate information about Tokyo. Covers
         geography, climate, housing, trade, transportation,
         education, food, customs, religion, sports, and problems.
         The text is readable and easy to understand. Illustrated
         with many black-and-white photographs, each of which has a
         short explanation. Included are a map of Tokyo, a glossary,
         an index, and a list of further readings.

7-094.   Maraini, Fosco and Editors of Time-Life Books. Tokyo. The
         Great Cities. Time-Life Books. Photographs by Harold Sund.
         Amsterdam: Time-Life International, c. 1976. 200 p. (7 up)

This excellent book depicts various aspects of this great, complex city in which modern culture and technology exist side-by-side with traditional culture. Excellent photographs and reproductions of wood block prints are accompanied by short essays in addition to the general text. Includes maps of Tokyo, a glossary, a bibliography, and an index.

7-095.   Miller, Elizabeth K. Tell Me about Tokyo. Illustrations by Yasuo Kazama. Rutland, VT: Tuttle, 1964. 39 p. (3-6)

The text is not very informative. Uses drawings instead of photographs as illustrations.

7-096.   Morton, W. Scott. The Japanese: How They Live and Work. How They Live and Work, New York: Praeger, 1973. 152 p. (9 up)

Written for businessmen and travelers to Japan, this book provides a great deal of information which would be useful to high school students studying Japan. The author presents his personal impressions of Japan in a readable text. Topics included are physical characteristics of the Japanese islands, government structure, industries, transportation, and leisure and cultural activities. Hints for visitors are also included. Index.

7-097.   Pezeu-Massabuau, Jacques. The Japanese Islands: A Physical and Social Geography. Translated and adapted from the French by Paul C. Blum. Rutland, VT: Tuttle, c. 1978. 283 p. (10 up)

The author analyzes Japan's history during the last 100 years in terms of the country's social and physical geography. The population of the country more than doubled after 1867 due primarily to the economic benefits of industrialization. The unfavorable physical environment of the Japanese islands with their small amount of cultivable land and meagre natural resources led Japan to look overseas for the land necessary to support the growing population. Despite its poor physical resources, Japan after World War II eventually became a formidable economic success. Pezeu-Massabuau attributes this success to the ability of Japanese of different social classes to work toward a common goal. Selected bibliography and index.

7-098.   Seidensticker, Edward. Low City, High City: Tokyo from Edo to the Earthquake. New York: Knopf, 1983. 302 p. (10 up)

The author, a well-known scholar and translator of Japanese literature, describes with affection and style the transformation of Edo, the Shogun's ancient capital, into Tokyo the modern metropolis. The period covered is the years between the end of the Tokugawa shogunate (1868) and the

great earthquake of September 1923. The numerous
illustrations, both color and black-and-white, are one of
the most valuable components of this book.

DAILY LIFE

7-099.   Aoki, Michiko and Dardess, Margaret B. eds. As the Japanese
          See It: Past and Present. Honolulu: The University Press
          of Hawaii, c. 1981. ix, 315 p. (10 up)

          This collection of readings is designed to present a picture
          of the daily life of ordinary people, to illustrate human
          concerns in Japanese society. The types of source material
          collected include folktales, excerpts from novels, short
          stories, journal and newspaper articles, and memoirs,
          interviews, and sermons. Many of the entries were translated
          for this collection. The book is divided into four parts--
          religion, family, community, and state--and each part
          contains several different kinds of sources. Useful
          collection. No index or bibliography.

7-100.   Bird, Isabella. Unbeaten Tracks in Japan. Rutland, VT:
          Tuttle, 1973. xxv, 336 p. (6 up)

          A fascinating series of letters written at the end of the
          nineteenth century by an American woman to a friend back
          home, which provide a view of ordinary life in rural Japan.
          Includes black-and-white illustrations of the time.
          Paperback.

7-101.   Bosworth, Allan R. The Lovely World of Richi-san. New York:
          Harper & Row, c. 1960. 222 p. (6 up)

          A true story of friendship among the author, an American
          naval officer stationed in Japan, and his Japanese friends,
          particularly Richi-san. A sensitive, warm story which is at
          the same time educational and informative. Explains numerous
          Japanese things, customs, and words accurately. Highly
          recommended reading for both fun and social studies.

7-102.   Carr, Rachel. The Picture Story of Japan. Picture Story
          Books of Other Countries. Illustrated by Kazue Mizumura.
          New York: McKay, c. 1962. 61 p. (3-6)

Young American children visit a Japanese home in Tokyo and
young children of the Japanese family explain their customs,
clothes, food, way of life and show their house to the
American children. Holidays, history, industries, sports,
and language are described very accurately and written in
easy-to-understand language. Extremely informative although
some of the customs explained here are disappearing.
Mizumura's good and charming illustrations add very much to
this good book for young readers. The book is old but good
and still useful, if available. Maps are included.

7-103.   Cavanna, Betty. Noko of Japan. Around the World Today Books
          Series. New York: Watts, 1964. 68 p. (4-6)

The life of a Japanese girl, Noko, is depicted. Noko does
not like to be a girl in Japan but later she learns there
are some good things about being one. Includes much
information about Japan. Many photographs.

7-104.   Cooper, Michael. ed. They Came to Japan: An Anthology of
          European Reports on Japan, 1543-1640. Berkeley: University
          of California Press, c. 1965, paperback edition 1981.
          xviii, 439 p. (9 up)

First-hand commentaries of thirty-five Europeans who came to
Japan during the sixteenth and seventeenth centuries. During
the first half-century after the Euopeans reached Japanese
shores, Japan was torn by internal warfare and was only
slowly reunified during the next half-century. This
collection provides valuable insight into Japan of that
time. The comments are grouped in chapters by topic.
Information can be found on such topics as geography,
history, castles, soldiers, law, language, food and drink,
dress, and cities.

7-105.   Darbois, Dominique. Noriko, Girl of Japan. Story and
          photographs by Dominique Darbois. Chicago: Follett, c.
          1964. 47 p. (3-4)

This book describes the daily life of a little girl, Noriko,
who lives in Kyoto, the ancient capital of Japan, but it has
a very stereotyped approach. It could be used as a companion
volume with Jun'ichi, a boy of Japan by Schloat (New York:
Knopf, 1964), but the latter is far more informative. Noriko
does not represent the average girl in present-day Japan.
Average children do not go to see No drama or Kabuki drama,
nor practice the koto (Japanese harp) the samisen (Japanese
stringed instrument), Japanese dancing, or flower arranging.
The photography is good and captures the flavor of both
modern and old Japan. Children will find this book
interesting since this girl could be one of their friends

because of her age, but they will also notice the difference and similarities in social life and customs. Includes a pronunciation chart.

7-106.   Dunn, C.J. _Everyday Life in Traditional Japan_. Drawings by Laurence Broderick. New York: Putnam's Sons, c. 1969. ix, 198 p. (9 up)

Everyday life during the Tokugawa period (1603-1867) is the focus of this book. Each chapter describes the typical life pattern of one social class. The classes covered are _samurai_, farmers, craftsmen, merchants, courtiers, priests, doctors and intellectuals, actors, and outcasts. One chapter is devoted to everyday life in Edo (Tokyo), the capital and center of political and social life in Tokugawa Japan. Illustrated with black-and-white drawings. Includes notes on further readings and a detailed index. Highly recommended.

7-107.   Epton, Nina. _Seaweed for Breakfast: A Picture of Japanese Life Today_. Illustrated with photographs. New York: Dodd, Mead, c. 1963. xiii, 268 p. (7 up)

The author lived with Japanese families of various social classes in different parts of the country. She relates many of the experiences she has had and describes the charm and friendliness of the people. The book is somewhat outdated, but there is still a good bit of valuable information about the way Japanese live.

7-108.   Fraser, Mary Crawford. _A Diplomat's Wife in Japan: Sketches at the Turn of the Century_. Edited by Hugh Cortazzi. New York: Weatherhill, c. 1982. xxxi, 351 p. (10 up)

This book is an edited version of the second edition of _A Diplomatist's Wife in Japan: Letters from Home to Home_, published in 1899. Mary Fraser was the wife of the head of the British legation to Japan at the end of the nineteenth century. The current British ambassador to Japan, Hugh Cortazzi, has edited her collection of letters and added an introduction to provide background for the modern reader. The text is easy to read and provides a valuable picture of Tokyo at the turn of the century. Fraser's understanding attitude, openness, and her sense of humor make this book enjoyable.

7-109.   Gidal, Sonia and Gidal, Tim. _My Village in Japan_. New York: Pantheon Books, A Division of Random House, c. 1966. 74 p. (4-66)

The text is readable and the photographs are good. Much of
the text is dialogue which contains inaccuracies in the use
of Japanese words and in the description of the behavior of
the participants in the conversation. Children do not bow to
their father every time their father says something.

7-110.   Hane, Mikiso. Peasants, Rebels, and Outcasts: The Underside
          of Modern Japan. New York: Pantheon Books, c. 1982. xiii,
          297 p. (10 up)

          This is a study of the effects which the drive to modernize
          Japan had on the lives of the common people. Using personal
          testimony, eyewitness accounts, memoirs, diaries, and
          individual recollections, the author provides a picture of
          the "lives and thoughts of the rural populace and of the
          poor who came out of the villages to enter the mines, the
          factories, and the brothels" during the period from 1868 to
          1942.

7-111.   Kirk, Ruth. Sigemi: A Japanese Village Girl. Photographs by
          Ira Spring. New York: Harcourt, c. 1965. 48 p. (3-6)

          This has a very accurate and informative text, with black-
          and-white photographs. It is an actual account of the way
          Sigemi, an eleven-year-old Japanese village girl, lives.
          Divided into three sections: family and village; school and
          play; and religion and festivals. The whole year's events in
          a Japanese village at the foot of Mt. Fuji are described and
          explained precisely.

7-112.   Lach, Donald F. Japan in the Eyes of Europe: The Sixteen
          Century. A Phoenix Book. Chicago: The University of
          Chicago Press, c. 1965 and 1968. p. 651-729. (12 up)

          This is a reproduction of one section of the author's major
          work, Asia in the Making (Chicago: 1965) and is intended to
          supplement standard histories of Japan. This work is based
          on the letters, histories, and other writings of the Jesuit
          missionaries and Portuguese merchants who were the first
          Westerners to come to Japan. The Jesuits, especially,
          relayed to Europe details about Japanese life and culture.
          It might surprise students to discover that by the end of
          the sixteenth century, about one-half century after being
          discovered, Japan was known by learned Europeans as a
          "united nation with an independent culture which rivaled and
          even excelled in some way the greatest states and cultures
          of Europe." An interesting and valuable book because of its
          special viewpoint and focus.

7-113.   Maki, John M. ed. We the Japanese: Voices from Japan. Voices
          from the Nations. New York: Praeger, 1972. 221 p. (9-12)

This is a lively collection of excerpts from a variety of Japanese sources by and about Japanese teenagers. The selections were taken from popular Japanese magazines for young people, from social studies textbooks, from government white papers on youth, and from a book written by a Japanese student who studied in the United States. All were translated specifically for this book. The topics treated include: life and society, politics and economics, young people and education, what an average Japanese ninth-grader is like, dating, social relations, delinquency, careers for young people, sports, and entertainment. This book contains much information not available in other sources.

7-114. Morris, Ivan. The World of the Shining Prince: Court Life in Ancient Japan. Penguin Books. Middlesex, England: Penguin Books, c. 1964. 348 p. (12 up)

Using The Tale of Genji as his source, Morris, in this intriguing book, analyzes court life in tenth- and eleventh-century Japan. Historical background is provided and topics such as politics, society, religion, superstition, and women are discussed. One chapter is devoted to Murasaki Shikibu, the author of The Tale of Genji. Various appendices include genealogical tables, a glossary, a bibliography, and an extensive index.

7-115. Neurath, Marie. They Lived Like This in Old Japan. Illustrated by Evelyn Worboys. New York: Watts, c. 1966. 32 p. (4-6)

All the illustrations in this book are based on ukiyoe prints of the eighteenth and nineteenth centuries, although the text talks about the eighth- to twelfth-century customs. Some of the illustrations are not authentic, and there are some mistakes and much stereotyping. Should be used with caution.

7-116. Rodrigues, Joao. This Land of Japon: Account of 16th-Century Japan. Translated and edited by Michael Cooper. New York: Kodansha International, c. 1973. 354 p. (10 up)

This account of sixteenth-century Japan was written by Joao Rodrigues, a Portuguese Jesuit priest who left his native country as a child, never to return, and lived in Japan for thirty-three years. The Japan which Rodrigues reached in 1577 was a country in a state of political and social transition, where all central authority had collapsed and civil war raged. Rodrigues worked as representative of the Jesuit mission and as an interpreter for visiting Portuguese merchants. He wrote home on a wide range of things Japanese, from ancient Japan to the tea ceremony. A very interesting book.

7-117.   Schloat, Warren. Jun'ichi: A Boy of Japan. New york: Knopf,
          c. 1964. Unpaged. (4-66)

          A detailed record of a day in the life of Jun'ichi, a
          twelve-year-old boy through the use of many black-and-white
          photographs. Jun'ichi's everyday life is depicted very well.
          The author paid close attention to the details of everyday
          life and as a result, the book is full of information not
          available elsewhere. A few aspects of daily life presented
          here have changed. Kerosine or gas stoves are now usually
          used to heat houses and the need for people to eat dried
          potatoes because of a shortage of rice has long disappeared.
          An unusually good, detailed, and informative book. Still
          highly recommended.

7-118.   Shirakigawa, Tomiko. Children of Japan. New York: Sterling,
          c. 1967. 95 p. (3-5)

          Divided into five parts: home life; school life; athletics;
          shrines and temples; and projects and pastimes. Very
          informative, includes many illustrations not available
          elsewhere. The occasional overstatement and inaccurate
          explanations are to be regretted.

7-119.   Sternberg, Martha. Japan: A Week in Daisuke's World.
          Photographs by Minoru Aoki. New York: Crowell-Collier,
          Macmillan, c. 1973. Unpaged. (K-2)

          A description of a normal week in the life of Daisuke, a
          seven-year-old Japanese boy. Nothing dramatic, but it is an
          accurate, good, and realistic description of an average
          Japanese boy's life in school and at home. Full of black-
          and-white photographs.

7-120.   Vining, Elizabeth Gray. Windows for the Crown Prince.
          Philadelphia: Lippincott, c. 1952. 320 p. (7 up)

          Mrs. Vining was invited to become a tutor to the Crown
          Prince in 1946. She remained Japan for several years and
          taught English to the Prince and to the Empress and her
          other children as well. This book records her impressions of
          Japan right after the war and provides a rare picture of
          life in the Imperial family.

7-121.   Whitney, Clara A.N. Clara's Diary: An American Girl in Meiji
          Japan. Edited by William Steele and Tamiko Ichimata. New
          York: Kodansha International, 1979. 353 p. (7 up)

          Fourteen-year-old Clara Whitney came to Japan in 1875 when
          her father was asked to help establish a national business
          college. Clara kept a diary from her arrival in Japan to the
          time of the birth of her first child by her Japanese husband

in 1884; she recorded Japanese life and customs as she saw them. Japan at that time was going through a period of rapid change and modernization and Clara's diary provides a vivid picture of the period and record of this change. The change in Clara's attitude toward the Japanese from one of Western ethnocentricism to sympathy and understanding is also evident.

7-122.   Worswick, Clark. ed. Japan: Photographs 1854-1905. Edited with a historical text by Clark Worswick. With an introduction by Jan Morris. New York: Pennwick/Knopf, 1979. 151 p. (9 up)

The main purpose of this book is to document the techniques and styles of Japanese photographers who worked between 1854 and 1905. Because this period is also the time when the Japanese set out to modernize their traditional feudal society, these 120 photographs provide an invaluable historical record of the time. Many are studio photographs.

FESTIVALS

7-123.   Buell, Hal. Festivals of Japan. New york: Dodd, Mead, c. 1965. 79 p. (4 up)

Excellent book for children on the festivals of Japan: accurate descriptions in a readable text. There is a good general introduction about Japan and its numerous festivals at the beginning of the book. Although in black and white, excellent and clear photographs are the strongest point of this book.

7-124.   Epstein, Sam and Epstein, Beryl. A Year of Japanese Festivals. Illustrated by Gordon Laite. Champaign, IL: Garrard, c. 1974. 96 p. (2-6)

This book lists various kinds of Japanese festivals, both of recent and ancient origin, and gives a detailed account for each festival. Unfortunately, some of the information is inaccurate, including some misspellings of Japanese words. Buell's book is much preferred.

7-125.   Haga, Hideo and Warner, G. Japanese Festivals. Osaka: Hoikusha, c. 1968. 1971. 127 p. (6 up)

Translation of one of the Hoikusha's Color Book Series:
<u>Nihon no Matsuri</u>. Not as complete as <u>Japanese Folk Festivals
Illustrated</u> (Haga, Tokyo: Miura Printing, 1970).

7-126.   Haga, Hideo. <u>Japanese Folk Festivals Illustrated</u>. Translated
          by Fanny Hagin Mayer. Tokyo: Miura Printing, 1970. 187 p.
          (6 up)

Descriptions and explanations of festivals are given. There
are many photographs, a large number of which are in color.
A festival calendar and map of Japan are appended. Very good
book.

7-127.   Soleillant, Claude. <u>Japan: Activities & Projects in Color</u>.
          New York: Sterling, c. 1980. 96 p. (3-9)

See ART, 1-027.

LANGUAGE AND TRAVEL

7-128.   Ashby, Gwynneth. <u>Take a Trip to Japan</u>. Take a Trip to
          Series. General editor Henry Pluckrose. New York: Watts,
          c. 1980. 32 p. (K-3)

Clear, color photographs, many of them taken by the author,
are accompanied by a short, easy-to-read text. The text is
informative but there is no organization whatsoever of the
information. Included are two maps -- one is a small, world
map showing where Japan is, and the other is a map of Japan
and the edge of the Continent of Asia. A list of words about
Japan includes thirty words; ten out of those are place
names. Words like incense, smoke, archery, scroll painting,
tea ceremony do not seem very productive in a book at this
level. Statements such as "Puppet shows are very popular" or
"Archery is a popular Japanese sports" makes one wonder
about the author's understanding of Japan.

7-129.   Geis, Darlene. <u>Let's Travel in Japan</u>. A Travel Press Book.
          Chicago: Childrens' Press, 1965. 85 p. (6 up)

Although this was published by the Childrens' Press in
Chicago and the format is that of a children's book, the
style of the text is very literary and would not be
tolerated by many young children. The majority of the

photographs have very clear color, and that is the strength
of this book. Includes a map, a brief chronology of Japanese
history, a list of Japanese words and phrases, and an index.

7-130.   Lifton, Betty Jean. A Dog's Guide to Tokyo. Photographs by
Eikoh Hosoe. New York: Norton, c. 1969. 64 p. (1-6)

Jumblie, a poodle, is the guide in this good and humorous
introduction to Japan. Good guidebook for young children as
well as for dogs! Illustrations are all in black and white,
but the photography, by a first-class Japanese photographer,
is excellent. Fairly informative.

7-131.   Maeda, Jun. Let's Study Japanese. Rutland, VT: Tuttle, 1965,
1978 printing. 130 p. (4 up)

This pocket-sized Japanese language book is intended for use
by tourists to Japan, but it could be used to acquire some
knowledge of the Japanese language. In twenty-six lessons,
it provides a basic vocabulary and includes a game and a
song. The many clear illustrations add to its classroom
usefulness.

7-132.   Morton, W. Scott. The Japanese: How They Live and Work. How
They Live and Work. New York: Praeger, 1973. 152 p. (9 up)

See GEOGRAPHY AND DESCRIPTION, 7-096.

7-133.   Murray, D.M. & Wong, T.W. Noodle Words: An Introduction to
Chinese and Japanese Characters. Rutland, VT: Tuttle, c.
1971. 95 p. (5 up)

The authors try to make the difficult task of learning
Chinese characters easier by making up silly stories and
jokes and they succeed in getting people involved by doing
so. Here is one example: the Chinese character for tortoise
really resembles a tortoise looked at from above or one seen
standing on its tail—whichever way you like to look at it;
to explain this character, the authors use a picture of a
tortoise standing on its tail and comments, "It was hard to
get the tortoise to stand on his tail like this--Confucius
(the supposed inventor of Chinese characters in this book)
had to sing the Chinese national anthem while he drew."
Generally the information in the book is accurate, and the
readers will have fun learning some of the characters. The
book is geared to people going to China or visiting a
Chinatown, although some sections like "Pictures and things"
and "A list of common radicals" can be used when studying
about Japan.

7-134.   Namioka, Lensey. Japan: A Traveler's Companion. New York:
Vanguard Press, c. 1979. x, 253 p. (6 up)

This travel book for tourists provides accurate, detailed information about Japan. Topics such as language, food, housing, amusements, sports, and arts and crafts are discussed. Appended with maps and suggested readings.

7-135.   Plutschow, Herbert. Introducing Kyoto. New York: Kodansha International, c. 1979. 72 p. (9 up)

A pictorial introduction to Kyoto which groups the photographs into two sections -- historical, and modern Kyoto. Each section is followed by a short essay. The essay on historical Kyoto covers the major historical buildings and their history. the essay on modern Kyoto deals primarily with festivals, and arts and crafts. There is a detailed map of Kyoto on one end paper and a chronology of Japanese history on the other.

7-136.   Seward, Jack. Japanese in Action. Revised ed. New York: Weatherhill, 1983. vii, 224 p. (10 up)

This is an advanced Japanese language text which also includes an abundance of information on the behavior and characteristics of the Japanese as a people. The author spent many years studying the Japanese language and lived in Japan over a quarter of a century. It is refreshing, humorous, interesting, and highly readable. Full of anecdotes and personal stories.

SAMURAI

7-137.   Allyn, John. The Forty-Seven Ronin Story. Rutland, VT: Tuttle, c. 1970. 240 p. (9 up)

See FICTION, 4-001.

7-138.   Carlson, Dade. Warlord of the Genji. Illustrated by John Gretzer. New York: Atheneum, 1970. 171 p. (5 up)

See FICTION, 4-010.

7-139.   Cocagnac, A.M. The Three Trees of the Samurai. Illustrated by Alain de Foll. New York: Harlin Quist, distributed by Dell, 1970. Unpaged. (2-6)

See DRAMA, 2-001.

7-140.   Draeger, Donn F. Ninjutsu: The Art of Invisibility. Japan's
         Feudal-Age Espionage Methods. Phoenix, AZ: Phoenix Books
         Publishers, c. 1980. 118 p. (9 up)

         A complete introduction to ninjutsu, a highly skilled
         martial art. Its history, training methods, and tools are
         clearly explained in the text and by illustrations.
         Intriguing book for someone interested in the general topic
         of martial arts.

7-141.   Gibson, Michael. The Samurai of Japan. Wayland Sentinel
         Book. London: Wayland publishers, c. 1973. 96 p. (5 up)

         This history of the samurai provides information on how
         samurai lived, their weapons and armor, and their philosophy
         from their rise during medieval Japan through the end of
         World War II. The positive aspects of the samurai way of
         life (their loyalty, courage, and sense of honor) are
         discussed as are the negative aspects. The modern samurai,
         the soldier in modern military service, is also considered.
         The text is interesting and accurate. The illustrations are
         generally good but some of them are mislabeled. (pages 24-
         25, 44-45, 50-51).

7-142.   Lewis, Brenda Ralph. Growing up in Samurai Japan. London:
         Batsford Academic and Educational, c. 1981. 72 p. (5 up)

         The information in this book is detailed and generally
         accurate, but there are some misspellings of Japanese words
         and some Japanese words are incorrectly defined or
         explained. Richly illustrated with art, drawings, and
         photographs. Includes a chronology, an index, and a
         glossary.

7-143.   Louis-Frederic. Daily Life in Japan at the Time of the
         Samurai. Translated from the French by Eileen M. Lowe.
         London: George Allen and Unwin, 1972. 256 p. (10 up)

         Originally published in French in 1967. Drawing from
         literature, historical sources, and paintings, the author
         was able to reconstruct the outlines of daily life in
         medieval Japan (1185-1603). Bibliography (includes English
         and Japanese material), an index, a list of shoguns, and a
         historical periods list. A good book for social studies.

7-144.   Macintyre, Michael. The Shogun Inheritance: Japan and the
         Legacy of the Samurai. London: Collins and British
         Broadcasting Corporation, 1982. 216 p. (10 up)

The author explains modern Japan in terms of its past. He argues that the samurai inheritance binds modern industrial Japan and its people. Half of the book is made up of large color photographs, and some of the explanations of the photographs seem farfetched and irrelevant.

7-145.   Storry, Richard. The Way of the Samurai. Photographs by
         Werner Forman. New York: Putnam's Sons, c. 1978. 128 p. (9
         up)

Detailed and vivid history of the samurai class, the warriors who dominated the power structure in Japan from the twelfth through the nineteenth centuries. Particularly interesting is the leadership role held by samurai in the modernization of the country. Storry sees the way of the samurai living on among the Japanese in a diluted form after the dismantling of the feudal society and feels that it required another revolution (the democratization of the country after World War II) to give the "ghosts of the samurai their final quietus." There are several mistakes in romanization. Appended with chronological tables, a glossary, notes, a bibliography, and an extensive index.

7-146.   Turnbull, Stephen R. A Book of the Samurai: The Warrior
         Class of Japan. London: Arms and Armour Press, c. 1982.
         192 p. (9 up)

This is the latest of this author's books on samurai. It is a history of the samurai class--their rise to power, how they lived and fought, and their eventual decline. Abundantly illustrated with large, exquisite, color reproductions of picture scrolls, wood-block prints, and photographs of arms and armor. The captions are very good, and the author often points out specifically what the reader should look for. Includes maps, a glossary, an index, and a bibliography. Illustration on page 165 is a doctor treating a woman patient, not a samurai.

7-147.   ----------------. The Samurai: A Military History. New York:
         Macmillan, c. 1977. 304 p. (10 up)

A comprehensive history of the military tradition in Japan from prehistory to the legal dissolution of the samurai class in the nineteenth century. Anecdotes, information on armor and swords, a discussion of samurai code of ethics as well as information on the economic status of the class are also included. An extensive, scholarly but readable history. Includes some genealogical tables, extensive bibliography and index. For the truly interested in this popular subject.

7-148.   ----------------. Warlords of Japan. Sampson Low Library of
         the Past. Maidenhead, England: Sampson Low, c. 1979. 48 p.
         (5-9)

         This book on samurai was written for a younger audience than
         the other two volumes described above. All aspects of
         samurai life are explained--everday life, education and
         training, warfare, religion, art, housing, sports and other
         pastimes. The text is informative and accurate except one
         small detail on page 33 about forty-seven ronin's suicide.
         After the revenge was completed, they turned themselves in,
         and awaited their sentence. They were ordered to die an
         honorable death, which is seppuku, disembowelment, and they
         were grateful for it.

SOCIETY

7-149.   Appel, Benjamin. Why the Japanese Are the Way They Are.
         Boston: Little, Brown, 1973. 151 p. (7 up)

         This attempt to interpret Japan to an American audience is
         simplistic and consequently inaccurate. The writing is also
         laden with the author's value judgements. There are no
         illustrations. Appended with maps and an index. Not
         recommended.

7-150.   Benedict, Ruth. The Chrysanthemum and the Sword: Patterns of
         Japanese Culture. Boston: Houghton Mifflin, c. 1946,
         paperback edition 1967. 324 p. (10 up)

         This is a classic work on Japanese behavior written by a
         cultural anthropologist during World War II. The author had
         never been to Japan and based her work on Japanese
         informants living in the United States, antiquarian papers
         written by Americans and Europeans about Japan, and her
         analysis of Japanese movies. The book "examines Japanese
         assumptions about the conduct of life, and it is about
         habits that are expected and taken for granted in Japan."
         The text is interesting and easy to read. There is a certain
         amount of overstatement but it is still "must" reading in
         Japanese studies. Glossary and index.

7-151.   Bernstein, Gail Lee. Haruko's World: A Japanese Farm Woman
         and Her Community. Stanford, CA: Stanford University
         Press, 1983. xvii, 199 p. (10 up)

This is a unique and important study of contemporary rural
Japanese women viewed primarily through the eyes of one
woman, Haruko. Haruko is a woman who lives with her husband,
mother-in-law, and two teenage children on a farm in a small
village on Shikoku, the smallest of the four main islands of
Japan. Many aspects of rural life are explored including
child rearing, education, effect of mechanization on the
people and the community, women's responsibilities and work,
social life and social organization. For the rural women,
"Just a housewife" is a dream and luxury. The author
explains, rightfully, that the difference in the aspirations
of women from different cultures and classes underscores the
need to place all social movements in both a cultural and
historical context. Very accurate and sensitive book. The
only small mistake found was that the author called the
salty plum inside of rice balls a cherry.

7-152.   Dalby, Liza Crihfield. Geisha. Berkeley, CA: University of
          California Press, c. 1983. xix, 347 p. (10 up)

In order to gain firsthand experience about geishas for her
doctoral dissertation, Dalby went through geisha training.
This book explores the place of the geisha in Japanese
culture and, in making the role and status of the geisha
clear, provides much information about Japanese customs,
history, law, psychology, male-female relationships, etc.
Well-written, intriguing study. Appended with detailed notes
and a glossary of Japanese words.

7-153.   Hane, Mikiso. Peasants, Rebels, and Outcasts: The Underside
          of Modern Japan. New York: Pantheon Books, c. 1982. xiii,
          297 p. (10 up)

See DAILY LIFE, 7-110.

7-154.   Hilger, M. Inez. Together With the Ainu: A Vanishing People.
          With the Assistance of Chiye Sano and Midori Yamaha.
          Norman, OK: University of Oklahoma Press, c. 1971. xxi,
          223 p. (7 up)

The Ainu are Caucasian-like aborigines whose ancestors once
occupied most, if not all, of the Japanese islands. Over the
centuries they have been pushed northward, and in modern
times exist as a cultural unit only on the northernmost
island of Hokkaido. The author, an American cultural
anthropologist, with the assistance of Japanese scholars and
with support from the Japanese government did an
ethnographic study of the Ainu from 1962 to 1963. This is
one of the very few contemporary sources available in
English on this minority group. Includes photographs with
short explanations, a glossary, an index, and a good
bibliography.

7-155.   Picken, Stuart D.B. Shinto, Japan's Spiritual Roots. New
         York: Kodansha International, 1980. 80 p. (10 up)

         An introduction to Japan's native religion. Good book with
         many excellent illustrations.

7-156.   Robins-Mowry, Dorothy. The Hidden Sun: Women of Modern
         Japan. With a Foreword by Edwin O. Reichauer. Boulder, CO:
         Westview Press, c. 1983. xxii, 394 p. (10 up)

         The author has analyzed how Japanese women view their role
         in modern society. As Women's Activities Officer in the U.S.
         Embassy in Tokyo from 1963 to 1971, she interviewed many
         Japanese women from every walk of life. There is a good
         historical overview of women in Japanese history, and the
         women's movements from the 1870s to the 1980s is studied in
         depth. The major part of the book is concerned with the
         changes in the role of women after World War II. Throughout
         the book, Japanese women speak for themselves through the
         inclusion of quotations from their memoirs, poetry, etc.
         Includes a chronology of events important to Japanese women,
         a list of the major women's organizations in Japan, an
         extensive bibliography, and an index. For advanced students.

7-157.   Sugimoto, Etsu. A Daughter of the Samurai. Rutland, VT:
         Tuttle, c. 1966, 1975 printing. xix, 314 p. (4 up)

         This is the biography of a Japanese woman who grew up in a
         warrior's family in the early decades of the twentieth
         century. She came to the United States as a young bride and
         remained here until after the death of her husband and then
         returned home with her two young daughters. Her description
         of her childhood is very interesting. The book was first
         published in 1926 and it is still very readable.

MODERN MIRACLE

7-158.   Axelbank, Albert. Japan Destiny. New York: Watts, c. 1973.
         107 p. (9 up)

         This book deals with Japan as a superpower and its problems
         in the 1970s. Many of the problems discussed are still
         problems in the 1980s. Topics dealt with include parties and
         politics, pacifism and patriotism, Japan and China, the

American legacy, and Japan in the twenty-first century.
Includes a chronology of Japan, a reading list, and an
index.

7-159.   Bolitho, Harold. Meiji Japan. Cambridge Topic Book.
          Published in cooperation with Cambridge University Press.
          Minneapolis: Lerner Publications, 1980. 48 p. (7 up)

          Originally published by Cambridge University Press in 1977.
          This book focuses on the latter half of the nineteenth
          century when Japan, pressured by the Western powers, was
          forced to modernize. The societal changes (political,
          economic, and social) required to bring about modernization
          and the problems the Japanese faced in making these changes
          are made clear, as are the effects the changes had on the
          lives of the Japanese people. Accurate and readable text
          with good maps and numerous illustrations. A welcome
          addition for the study of Japan at the junior high and high
          school levels.

7-160.   Burks, Ardath W. Japan: Profile of Postindustrial Power.
          Boulder, CO: Westview Press, 1981. xii, 260 p. (10 up)

          This is a much broader survey of Japan than the title
          implies. Two-thirds of the book provides a very good
          introduction to the geography, history, and culture of
          Japan. The remainder of the book focuses on modern Japan as
          a postindustrial society, that is, a society in which the
          knowledge-intensive sector of the economy (trade, finance,
          management, information retrieval, etc.) absorbs most of the
          labor and generates most of the income. Comparisons are made
          between the Japanese and U.S. approach to the problems this
          new kind of society presents. The social and economic
          organization of Japan is discussed as well as the problems
          Japan faces as a member of the international community.

7-161.   Grossberg, Kenneth A. ed. Japan Today. Philadelphia:
          Institute for the Study of Human Issues, c. 1981. 118 p.
          (10 up)

          Ten papers from a series of conferences held in the United
          States on "Japan Today" are included here in somewhat
          abbreviated form. They offer a concise and comprehensive
          overview of Japan today and tomorrow.

7-162.   Roberts, John G. Industrialization of Japan. New York:
          Watts, c. 1971. 88 p. (5 up)

          Good, accurate, introduction to the industrial modernization
          of Japan. Written in clear English, it includes a glossary
          and an index. Unfortunately, the black-and-white
          illustrations are often not clear.

7-163.   Taylor, Jared. <u>Shadows of the Rising Sun: A Critical View of</u>
          <u>the "Japanese Miracle."</u> New York: Morrow, 1983. 336 p. (10
          up)

The purpose of the book is to help Americans understand why
Japan has become a successful competitor on the
international level. The author, who was brought up in
Japan, describes Japanese society critically and explains
how the rigid hierarchization of society, the tendency
toward conformity, submission to group, xenophobia and race
consciousness have contributed to the present character of
Japan. Taylor believes that the single most important
ingredient in Japan's success is the Japanese attitude
toward work. The book makes a unique contribution to the
understanding of the "Japanese miracle." It will certainly
provoke many interesting discussions. A very fair and just
account of modern Japan.

7-164.   Trager, James. <u>Letters from Sachiko: A Japanese Woman's View</u>
          <u>of Life in the Land of the Economic Miracle.</u> New York:
          Atheneum, 1982. 218 p. (10 up)

The book is written in the form of letters from a Japanese
woman to her sister in the United States. The letters deal
with everyday matters and are very useful to learn about the
position and role of women in Japan. This book tells what it
is like to be a woman, especially a housewife, in this
economically strong country. Accompanied with detailed notes
including a section on why it costs Detroit much more money
to produce a small, well-built car than it costs Japanese
automobile manufacturers. Generally, the notes explain
Japanese words, give background information, or point out
things the reader might not otherwise notice. An index.

BOOKS TO BUILD BACKGROUND

Benedict, Ruth.   Chrysanthemum and the Sword: Patterns of
                               Japanese Culture. Boston: Houghton
                               Mifflin, c. 1946. 324 p.

Christopher, Robert C.   The Japanese Mind: The Goliath Explained.
                               New York: Linden Press, 1983. 352 p.

Hall, John Whitney.   Japan: From Prehistory to Modern Times.
                               New York: Dell, c. 1970. xii, 397 p.

-------------------.   Twelve Doors to Japan. By John Whitney
                               Hall and Richard K. Beardsley. New York:
                               McGraw-Hill, 1965. xxi, 649 p.

Reischauer, Edwin O.   The Japanese. Cambridge, MA: The Berknap
                               Press of Harvard University Press, 1977.
                               443 p.

Varley, H. Paul.   Japanese Culture. Third ed. Honolulu:
                               University of Hawaii Press, c. 1984, 331
                               p.

GLOSSARY

Ainu	Caucasian-like aborigine of Japan
Amano Jaku	A mischievous goblin who opposes whatever others say or do
Baku	A mythical animal which lives on bad dreams
Biwa	Japanese lute
Bushido	The samurai or knightly code
Daruma	A red papièr-maché tumbler doll representing Buddhidharma
Geisha	Professional entertainer and beauty
Geta	Japanese wooden footgear
Giri	A sense of duty and obligation
Hai	Yes
Haiku	A seventeen syllable poem
Hara-kiri	See Seppuku
Hibachi	A charcoal brazier used for heating
Hina	Doll
Imo	A long, edible root like a yam
Jinrikisha	Rickshaw
Jizo	Guardian deity of the people
Kabuki	Highly-stylized Japanese traditional drama performed exclusively by male actors
Kaidan	Scary tales
Kamishibai	Picture-card show
Kappa	A mythical water imp with a child's body and webbed hands and feet. It has a flat plate filled with water on its head which is the source of its power.
Kimono	Traditional Japanese costume for both men and women
Koto	Japanese zither
Kozo	Priestling
Kwaidan	See Kaidan
Kyogen	Comical farce played between No plays
Ninjo	Human feelings

Ninjutsu	Art of invisibility. Highly skilled martial art traditional in Japan, of stealing into enemy's territory or camp using various tricks
No	Traditional Japanese drama with extremely stylized acting. The actors wear symbolic masks and perform to special music and singing. The themes of the plays are solemn usually.
Obaasan	Grandmother
Obasan	Aunt, lady or woman
Origami	Japanese paper folding
Oshosan	Buddhist priest in charge of a temple
Otosan	Father
Ronin	Masterless samurai warrior in the feudal period
Samisen	See Shamisen
Samurai	Warrior class of feudal Japan. For 700 years, this class provided the social and political as well as the military leadership for Japan.
Seppuku	A ritual suiside by disembowelment. Considered to be the honorable way of dying for the samurai class instead of being handed over to a common executioner.
Shamisen	Traditional three-string Japanese musical instrument
Shogun	Supreme Japanese military leader of the feudal period who governed in the emperor's name.
Sumie	Black and white painting using India ink
Sumo	Japanese traditional-style wrestling
Tanishi	A mud snail considered to be messenger of the water god
Tanka	See Waka
Tanuki	A raccoon dog, or a kind of badger, which is said to play tricks on people, but its tricks are simpler and less harmful than those of foxes
Tengu	A long-nosed, red-raced mythical creature and human in form. Lives deep in the mountains and has supernatural powers and a round magic fan made of feathers.
Tofu	Soy-bean curd
Tombo	Dragonfly
Tsuru	Crane
Ukiyoe	Colored woodblock prints of the 17th through the 19th centuries which depict the flourishing urban life of the times
Waka	Japanese verse of thirty-one syllables
Warabe uta	Nursery songs
Yakuza	Gangster, the Japanese mafia
Zori	Japanese sandals

AUTHOR INDEX

TITLE INDEX

www.ingramcontent.com/pod-product-compliance
Lightning Source LLC
Chambersburg PA
CBHW050229270326
41914CB00003BA/633